WHEN GODS MUST RETURN

When Gods Must Return

Darwin Garg

Contents

To my parents,
who gave me the Gods before I knew I needed them.
To my wife, Urja,
whose belief in this book never wavered, even when
mine did.
And to Vihaan and Nirvaan,
you are my greatest reason for everything.

Introduction

The world feels like it's breaking.

Information floods overwhelm us daily - we can't tell truth from lies, real from manufactured, signal from noise. Mental health crises touch nearly every family. The climate emergency accelerates while we watch. Authoritarianism rises across democracies we thought were stable. Inequality grows to levels that threaten social fabric. Institutions we trusted reveal themselves as corrupt. Technology that promised connection delivers isolation and addiction. We face impossible choices where every option violates something we hold sacred.

These aren't separate crises but interconnected symptoms of systems designed for an age that's ending and a way of being human that's no longer sustainable.

And yet, thousands of years ago, ancient wisdom anticipated exactly these challenges. Not in their modern forms - the ancients didn't know about AI or social media or climate models - but in their essential patterns. The human struggles we face today aren't new. They're timeless. And timeless wisdom speaks to them with surprising clarity.

This book explores ten forms of that wisdom through the lens of the *Dashavatar* - the ten avatars of Vishnu from Hindu tradition. Each avatar represents a different kind of wisdom, a different capacity we need to navigate life's challenges. And each speaks directly to a crisis we're facing right now.

But here's the insight that makes this more than just ten separate teachings: **The avatars need each other.** They're not alternatives where you pick the one that fits your situation. They're an integrated whole, each essential, each incomplete without the others. This book builds toward that understanding - that facing the complexity of modern life requires all ten forms of wisdom working together.

The Ten Avatars and Ten Crises

In Hindu tradition, Vishnu takes ten forms (avatars) to protect and preserve *dharma* - cosmic order, righteousness, the way things should be - when it's threatened. Each avatar addresses a specific kind of crisis in a specific way.

We'll explore these ten avatars through ten modern crises:

Matsya (the fish who saved humanity from a great flood) speaks to our information crisis - how do we navigate floods of misinformation and preserve truth?

Kurma (the tortoise who provided stable foundation) speaks to our mental health crisis - how do we build inner stability when everything feels chaotic?

Varaha (the boar who rescued the earth) speaks to environmental destruction - how do we reconnect with and protect what sustains life?

Narasimha (the half-lion who defeated a tyrant) speaks to authoritarianism - how do we resist abuse of power?

Vamana (the dwarf who taught humility to an arrogant king) speaks to ego and inequality - how do we recognize our appropriate limits?

Parashurama (the warrior who dismantled corrupt systems) speaks to institutional corruption - how do we address rot in our structures?

Rama (the prince who chose integrity over comfort) speaks to ethical erosion - how do we do what's right when it costs everything?

Krishna (who counseled action in impossible dilemmas) speaks to complex moral situations - how do we choose when there's no right answer?

Buddha (who understood craving and suffering) speaks to addiction - how do we break free from cycles we can't seem to stop?

Kalki (the future avatar of transformation) speaks to systemic change - how do we transform systems that create these crises?

Each avatar offers essential wisdom. But the book's core message is that you need all ten - not one at a time, but integrated and working together. Life's complexity requires nothing less.

What This Book Is

This is a book about ancient wisdom applied to modern life. It uses Hindu mythology as a framework, but it's written for everyone - regardless of your religious background or lack thereof. You don't need to be Hindu to find value here, nor any prior knowledge of these stories.

This is accessible wisdom, not academic theology. The tone is conversational, like a thoughtful friend sharing insights over coffee. The approach is practical - each chapter offers not just philosophy but actionable guidance.

This is a book that respects both the ancient tradition and your intelligence. The mythology is presented faithfully but interpreted for modern application. The wisdom is honored but not treated as dogma.

What This Book Isn't

This isn't a religious text trying to convert you to Hinduism; its wisdom literature drawing on Hindu tradition.

This isn't an academic treatise. There are no footnotes, no Sanskrit technical terms, no scholarly debates about textual interpretation. Those things have their place, but not here.

This isn't a definitive theological statement. Hindu tradition is vast, diverse, and contains multiple interpretations of these stories. This book offers one interpretation – mine – focused on practical wisdom for modern challenges. Other interpretations are equally valid.

This isn't a self-help book promising quick fixes. The wisdom here is real, but it's not easy. It requires practice, failure, learning, and trying again. There are no "five simple steps" to transformation.

This isn't only for people in crisis but also for people who want to understand the world we're living in, who want wisdom for challenges they haven't faced yet, who want to develop capacities they'll need for an uncertain future.

How to Read This Book

The book has eleven chapters. Chapters 1-10 each focus on one avatar and one modern crisis. Chapter 11 brings them all together, showing why they must coexist and what becomes possible when they do.

You can read sequentially - starting with Chapter 1 and moving through to Chapter 11. This lets you see how each avatar's limitations point to the need for the next, building toward the synthesis.

Or you can jump to what resonates - if you're facing a particular crisis right now, start with that chapter. Each chapter stands alone. You don't need to read them in order, though you'll eventually want to read Chapter 11 to see how they integrate.

Each chapter follows a similar structure:

- Opens with a modern character facing a crisis
- Explores the broader pattern of that crisis in contemporary life
- Tells the avatar's story from Hindu mythology

- Bridges ancient wisdom to modern application
- Offers practical guidance you can use
- Acknowledges the avatar's limitations, pointing toward the need for other wisdom

The chapters are written to be engaging, not exhausting. They use real characters and situations you can relate to. The mythology is told as story, not lecture. The wisdom is offered as invitation, not prescription.

A Note on Mythology

These avatar stories come from Hindu tradition - primarily the Puranas, the *Mahabharat*, and the *Ramayan*. They're ancient, sacred texts that billions of people revere.

I approach them with deep respect but not as literal history or unquestionable doctrine. I treat them as wisdom literature – stories that contain profound insights about human nature, ethical dilemmas, and what it means to live well.

My interpretations focus on practical wisdom for modern life. Traditional Hindu scholars might interpret these stories differently. That's not only okay - it's how living traditions work. Multiple interpretations can coexist, each offering different insights.

If you're Hindu and find my interpretations resonate, wonderful. If you're Hindu and interpret these stories differently, that's equally wonderful. If you're not Hindu and these stories are new to you, welcome – they have wisdom for you too.

The goal isn't to provide the definitive understanding of these avatars. The goal is to make their wisdom accessible and applicable to the challenges we're all facing, regardless of our religious backgrounds.

What I Hope You'll Gain

I hope you'll finish this book with a richer understanding of the crises we're facing - not as isolated problems but as interconnected challenges requiring integrated wisdom.

I hope you'll discover capacities within yourself you didn't know you had - Matsya's discernment, Kurma's stability, Varaha's fierce care, Narasimha's courage, Vamana's humility, Parashurama's persistence, Rama's integrity, Krishna's wisdom, Buddha's peace, Kalki's transformative vision.

I hope you'll see that ancient wisdom isn't obsolete – it speaks powerfully to our modern moment, offering guidance our contemporary culture often lacks.

Most importantly, I hope you'll understand that you need all ten forms of wisdom, not just one or two. That facing life's complexity requires multiple capacities working together. That the goal isn't to master one avatar but to integrate all ten.

The world needs people who can navigate information floods while maintaining inner stability while protecting what's sacred while resisting tyranny while practicing humility while persisting through difficulty while maintaining integrity while navigating complexity while finding peace while working for transformation.

The world needs people who are developing all ten capacities. People like you.

The Journey

This book is an invitation to a journey. Not a quick journey with a clear destination, but a lifelong practice of developing wisdom.

The avatars aren't just ancient stories. They're capacities within you that you can develop. Matsya's discernment is your discernment. Kurma's stability is your stability. All ten are available to you, right now, if you choose to develop them.

The work won't be easy. But it will be worthwhile. Because the crises we're facing aren't going away. They're getting more intense. And we need people who are developing the wisdom to face them – not just to survive but to help others survive, not just to navigate but to transform, not just to endure but to flourish.

That's what this book offers. Not answers, but wisdom. Not solutions, but capacities. Not certainty, but guidance for uncertainty.

The avatars have been waiting for thousands of years. They're ready to meet you.

Let's begin.

1

Matsya - When Truth Drowns

It's 11:47 PM, and Maya can't sleep.

She's been scrolling for twenty minutes—or was it an hour? Her phone screen glows blue in the darkness, and her thumb moves almost automatically: swipe, tap, scroll, swipe. A headline about a new virus. A video claiming vaccines cause infertility. A thread explaining why the video is wrong. Another thread explaining why the first thread is propaganda. A celebrity died—no wait, that's fake news. Or is it? Someone's already posted a "fact-check" but the comments say the fact-checkers are bought and paid for.

Her chest tightens. She just wanted to know if she should get her daughter vaccinated next week – one simple question. But now, twenty browser tabs later, she's more confused than when she started. Half the internet says one thing; half says the opposite. Everyone sounds confident. Everyone has sources. Everyone calls the other side liars.

Maya puts the phone down. Picks it up again thirty seconds later.

She remembers when her mother had questions, she'd call the doctor, go to the library, ask a trusted elder. There was an answer, usually. Or at least a clear path to finding one. Now? Now Maya has access to every piece of information humanity has ever produced, at her fingertips, instantly—and she's never felt more lost.

Welcome to the flood.

Not a flood of water, but something just as devastating: a deluge of information, misinformation, and everything in between. We're drowning in data while dying of thirst for truth. Every day, we're hit by tsunamis of news, opinions, facts, lies, half-truths, and propaganda, all mixed together, all demanding our attention, all insisting they alone hold the answer.

And we're exhausted.

We can't tell what's real anymore. We don't know who to trust. We're paralyzed by too many choices and terrified of making the wrong one. We're connected to billions of people but more confused than ever about what's actually happening in the world.

The flood isn't coming. We're already underwater.

But here's what's remarkable: this isn't the first time humanity has faced a flood that threatened to destroy everything...

The Modern Crisis

The flood takes many forms.

There's the morning flood: you wake up, check your phone, and before your feet hit the floor, you've already consumed forty-seven headlines, thirteen notifications, six texts, and a barrage of emails. Your brain is making decisions—what to read, what to ignore, what to believe—before you've even brushed your teeth.

There's the social media flood: your cousin shares an article about corruption in government. It has charts, statistics, quotes from officials. Looks legitimate. You share it. Two hours later, someone comments that it's from a satirical site. Or worse—it's real, but the statistics are manipulated. Or worse still—the statistics are accurate, but they're missing context that completely changes the meaning. You delete your post, embarrassed. How were you supposed to know?

There's the expert flood: remember when we trusted doctors, scientists, journalists? Now for every expert saying one thing, there's another expert—with equally impressive credentials—saying the opposite. Climate scientists warn of catastrophe; other scientists call it exaggerated. Nutritionists say eat this; other nutritionists say it'll kill you. Everyone has studies. Everyone has data. Who's right?

There's the urgency flood: everything is BREAKING NEWS. Everything is a crisis. Everything demands your immediate attention and outrage. Wars, scandals, injustices, conspiracies—they pour in relentlessly, each one screaming that if you don't pay attention RIGHT NOW, you're complicit, you're ignorant, you're part of the problem.

And perhaps most insidious, there's the algorithmic flood: the platforms we use to navigate information have learned what keeps us engaged. Not what informs us. Not what's true. What keeps us clicking. So, they feed us what confirms what we already believe, what triggers our emotions, what keeps us scrolling. We think we're seeking truth; we're actually trapped in personalized whirlpools of content designed to hold our attention, not expand our understanding.

The result? We're paralyzed.

A father wants to know if a new medication is safe for his son. He finds seventeen articles saying yes, nineteen saying no, and twenty-three saying "it depends." He makes no decision, frozen by conflicting certainty.

A young woman wants to understand what's happening in a war halfway across the world. She watches footage that breaks her heart—but is it real? Is it from this conflict or another? Is it recent or recycled? Has it been edited? She doesn't know. She feels guilty for doubting, guilty for believing, guilty for doing nothing.

A teacher wants to educate her students about history. But whose history? Which version? She's accused of bias no matter what she teaches. The textbooks contradict each other. Parents demand different narratives. Truth feels like whatever perspective shouts loudest.

We've built a world where everyone can speak, and no one can be heard. Where information is infinite, and knowledge is scarce. Where we're connected to everything, and understand nothing.

This is not progress. This is drowning.

And the water keeps rising.

The First Flood

Thousands of years ago, in a time before memory, there was another flood.

Not of information, but of water. Not digital, but devastatingly real. And humanity was just as lost, just as terrified, just as certain they were about to be destroyed.

The story goes like this:

A king named Manu was performing his morning rituals at the river. He cupped water in his hands, and in it, a tiny fish appeared. The fish spoke—yes, spoke—and said, "Protect me, and I will protect you."

Manu could have dismissed it. A talking fish? Clearly he was imagining things. Clearly this made no sense. But something in him listened. He took the fish home, placed it in a jar.

The fish grew. Overnight, it outgrew the jar. Manu moved it to a pond. It outgrew the pond. He moved it to a lake. It outgrew the lake. Finally, Manu released it into the ocean, and the fish revealed itself: this was no ordinary creature. This was Matsya—Vishnu himself, in the form of a fish.

And Matsya brought a warning: "A great flood is coming. It will destroy everything. Build a boat. Gather the seeds of every plant, two of every animal, the seven sages, and the sacred texts. When the waters rise, I will come for you."

Manu listened. While others dismissed the warning—how could the whole world flood? Where would all that water come from? This is absurd!—Manu built his boat. He gathered what needed to be preserved. He prepared.

And the flood came.

The rains fell. The oceans rose. The world as humanity knew it disappeared beneath churning, endless water. Everything was chaos. No landmarks. No direction. No way to tell up from down, safe from dangerous, truth from illusion. Just water, everywhere, overwhelming and absolute.

And in that chaos, Matsya appeared.

Massive now, magnificent, a golden fish the size of a mountain. Manu tied his boat to Matsya's horn, and the fish guided them through the deluge. Not by stopping the flood—that was impossible. But by navigating it. By knowing which direction to go when all directions looked the same. By moving with purpose when everything else was random destruction.

Matsya didn't save everyone. Most of humanity perished. But what mattered—the knowledge, the seeds of life, the wisdom worth preserving—survived. When the waters finally receded, Manu and the sages stepped onto new land and began again.

Humanity was reborn. Not because the flood was prevented, but because someone knew how to navigate it.

Navigating Our Flood

Do you see it now?

We are Manu, standing at the river, overwhelmed by what's coming. The flood of information isn't going to stop. If anything, it's going to get worse. More platforms, more AI-generated content that sounds authoritative, more sophisticated manipulation, more noise drowning out signal.

We can't stop it. Just like Manu couldn't stop the rains.

But we can learn to navigate it.

Look at what Manu did—and more importantly, what he didn't do. He didn't try to fight the flood. He didn't build walls to hold back the ocean. He didn't deny it was coming or pretend everything would be fine. He didn't freeze in panic or drown in despair.

He listened to the small voice of truth when it appeared. He prepared. He discerned what was worth preserving. And when the chaos came, he trusted a guide who could see clearly when he could not.

This is what Matsya teaches us about surviving information overload: discernment, preparation, and guidance.

First, discernment

Manu had to decide: is this talking fish real, or am I losing my mind? In a world where fish don't talk, believing this one did was absurd. But Manu didn't dismiss it reflexively. He tested it. He watched the fish grow. He paid attention to whether its actions matched its words. And when the evidence mounted, he trusted what he was seeing, even though it defied convention.

We need this same quality now. Not blind belief. Not automatic skepticism. But active discernment—the ability to test what we hear, to watch for consistency, to notice when something rings true versus when it just rings loud.

When Maya scrolled through those vaccine articles at midnight, what she needed wasn't more information. She needed discernment. The ability to ask: Who benefits from this message? What's the source's track record? Does this appeal to my fear or my reason? Is this clarifying or confusing? Does this guide me toward truth or just toward more clicking?

Second, preservation

Manu didn't try to save everything. He couldn't fit the whole world on his boat. He had to choose: What actually matters? What's worth preserving when everything else is washed away?

He chose seeds—the potential for new growth. He chose the sages—carriers of wisdom. He chose the sacred texts—the accumulated knowledge of generations. He let go of everything else.

We're drowning partly because we're trying to consume everything. Every article. Every opinion. Every update. We treat all information as equally important, so we're crushed by the sheer volume.

But it's not all equally important.

What are the seeds in your information diet? The sources that consistently help things grow in your understanding? What are your sages—the voices who have earned your trust over time, who admit when they're wrong, who care about truth more than clicks? What are your sacred texts—the foundational knowledge that doesn't change with every trending topic?

Identify these. Prioritize these. Let the rest of the flood pass by.

Third, guidance

Here's what's humbling about Manu's story: even after he prepared, even after he discerned truth from delusion, he couldn't navigate the flood alone; he needed Matsya. He needed someone who could see clearly when everything around him was chaos.

We need this too. Not gurus who demand blind obedience. Not algorithms that feed us what keeps us engaged. But genuine guides—people, institutions, practices that help us navigate when we're lost.

Maybe it's a journalist who's been consistently reliable. Maybe it's a friend who thinks differently than you but in good faith. Maybe it's a practice of stepping back before sharing, of reading the full article not just the headline, of asking "what would I need to know to prove this wrong?" before accepting it as fact.

The point is this: you can't navigate this flood purely on your own instincts. The waters are too chaotic. You need something outside yourself to hold onto, something that stays steady when everything else is churning.

What Matsya Would Do Today

So what does this actually look like in practice? How do you become Matsya in your own life—the one who navigates clearly while others drown?

The ancient fish-god offers us timeless practices, dressed now in modern clothes:

Build your boat before the storm

Don't wait until you're in crisis to figure out what you trust. Manu built his boat before the rains came. You need to build your information infrastructure now, while you're calm and thinking clearly.

This means: Identify three to five sources you'll turn to first when you need reliable information on important topics. Not sources that tell you what you want to hear—sources that have proven over time that they care about accuracy. Maybe it's a specific journalist. A particular publication. A trusted friend who's knowledgeable in an area. A professional organization in a field.

Write them down. Literally. When the next crisis hits and you're panicked and everyone's screaming contradictory things, you'll have your boat ready. You'll know where to go first.

Practice the pause

Matsya didn't rush. The story emphasizes his steady guidance through chaos. There's wisdom in slowness when everything around you is frantic.

Before you share that outrageous article, pause. Before you make a decision based on something you just read, pause. Before you let a headline ruin your day, pause.

Ask yourself: Do I need to have an opinion on this right now? Do I need to share this immediately? What would I lose by waiting an hour, a day, a week to see if this holds up?

The flood wants you reactive. Matsya teaches you to be responsive—there's a difference.

Learn to recognize your fish

Remember, Matsya started small. A tiny fish in cupped hands. Truth often appears this way—small, easy to dismiss, asking for protection in a world that might destroy it.

Pay attention to the quiet voices that prove themselves over time. The friend who admits when they're wrong. The source that says "we don't know yet" instead of jumping to conclusions. The perspective that challenges you but does so respectfully, with evidence.

These are your fish. Protect them. Don't let the flood drown them out.

Curate ruthlessly

Manu couldn't save everything, and neither can you. Every app you have, every account you follow, every newsletter you subscribe to—it's all adding to your flood.

Do a brutal audit. What actually helps you understand the world better? What just makes you anxious, angry, or confused? What claims to inform you but really just entertains or enrages you?

Unfollow. Unsubscribe. Delete. Be ruthless. You're not building an ark for everything—you're preserving what matters.

This isn't about creating an echo chamber. It's about the difference between signal and noise. Keep the voices that challenge you with substance. Cut the ones that just add to the chaos.

Create sacred reading time

The sages on Manu's boat didn't just carry wisdom—they created space for it. You need this too.

Set aside time—even fifteen minutes a day—for deeper reading. Not scrolling. Not skimming headlines. Actually reading something substantial, something that requires thought.

This is countercultural. Everything in our information environment is designed for quick hits, for skimming, for rapid consumption. Resist it. Deep reading is how you build the mental strength to navigate shallow waters.

Find your community of navigators

Manu didn't sail alone. He had the sages with him—a community of people committed to preserving truth and wisdom.

You need this. Find people—online or in person—who are also trying to navigate the flood thoughtfully. Not people who all agree with you, but people who share your commitment to seeking truth over winning arguments.

This might be a book club that reads deeply on important topics. A group of friends who've agreed to fact-check each other kindly. An online community that values nuance over hot takes.

When you're surrounded by people trying to think clearly, it becomes easier to think clearly yourself.

Trust the process, not the panic

Finally, remember: Matsya didn't promise to prevent suffering. The flood still came. Most of humanity still perished. But what mattered survived and grew again.

You won't get everything right. You'll believe things that turn out to be false. You'll miss important information. You'll be fooled sometimes. This is inevitable.

But if you're practicing discernment, preserving what matters, and following reliable guides, you'll navigate through. The goal isn't perfection. It's survival and growth.

The flood will recede eventually. New patterns will emerge. But only if enough of us learn to navigate rather than drown.

What Matsya Cannot Do

But here's what we need to be honest about: even if we all became perfect navigators of information, even if we could discern truth from lies with perfect accuracy, even if we preserved only what mattered and followed only trustworthy guides—we would still be in crisis.

Because the flood of misinformation is a symptom, not the disease.

Think about it: Why is there so much misinformation in the first place? Because people in power benefit from confusion. Because institutions have become corrupt and lost our trust. Because we're so anxious and unstable inside that we grasp at whatever makes us feel certain. Because our egos need to be right more than they need to be truthful. Because we're addicted to the dopamine hit of outrage and validation. Because we've lost our ethical compass and don't know what's worth standing for anymore.

Matsya can help you navigate the flood. But he can't address why the flood exists. He can't fix the authoritarians who weaponize misinformation. He can't heal the corruption in institutions that makes us distrust everything. He can't cure the inner instability that makes us vulnerable to manipulation. He can't humble the egos that spread lies for personal gain.

Navigation is essential. But it's not enough.

Manu survived the flood and stepped onto new land—but then what? He still had to build a new world. He still had to address the problems that caused the flood in the first place. He still needed wisdom beyond survival.

So do we.

You can learn to discern truth, but if you're too mentally exhausted and lonely to act on it, what good is it? You can identify reliable guides, but if those guides are silenced by tyrants, where does that leave you? You can preserve what matters, but if environmental collapse destroys the world, what will you preserve it for?

The information crisis is real. Learning to navigate it is crucial. But it's only one piece of a much larger puzzle.

This is why we need more than Matsya.

We need the patience and stability of Kurma when our minds are too fractured to think clearly. We need the fierce protective power of Narasimha when tyrants try to control what we can know. We need the humility of Vamana to counter the egos that create misinformation for profit and glory. We need Rama's unwavering ethics when we're tempted to fight lies with lies. We need Krishna's wisdom for the complex moral choices that perfect information won't solve. We need Buddha's teaching on detachment when we're addicted to the flood itself.

Matsya saves us from drowning. But survival is just the beginning.

The question isn't just "How do we navigate the flood?" It's "What world do we build when we reach the other shore?"

And that requires every avatar, working together, addressing every crisis at once.

Starting with the crisis within ourselves.

* * *

2

Kurma - The Search for Solid Ground

The notification sounds at 3:14 AM, and Sarah's eyes snap open.

She reaches for her phone before she's even fully conscious. A like on the photo she posted six hours ago. She exhales. Opens Instagram. Scrolls. Her anxiety lessens slightly—the photo has forty-three likes now. Good. Not great, but good enough. She checks the comments. Someone she barely knows from high school wrote "cute!" with a heart emoji. She smiles in the darkness.

Then she sees it: her friend Emma posted about getting promoted. The photo shows Emma at a celebratory dinner, surrounded by friends, wine glasses raised, everyone laughing. Sarah's stomach tightens. Emma got promoted – again. Emma's always getting promoted. Emma has her life together. Emma probably sleeps through the night instead of checking her phone at 3 AM like some kind of—

Sarah closes Instagram. Opens TikTok. Just for a minute. Just to calm down.

Forty minutes later, she's watched seventeen videos about productivity hacks, twelve about morning routines of successful people, eight about why she's probably depressed (she screenshots those), and twenty-three that are just... nothing. Funny. Distracting. Each one delivers a tiny hit of something that feels like relief but isn't.

Her alarm goes off at 6:30. She's been awake for three hours but feels like she hasn't slept at all. She drags herself out of bed, already exhausted, already behind, already comparing herself to everyone who seems to have it more together than she does.

By 9 AM, she's had two cups of coffee and still can't focus on the report that's due at noon. Her mind is racing but going nowhere. Anxious about everything, motivated by nothing. She knows she should meditate—she's downloaded four different meditation apps—but she can't sit still long enough. She knows she should exercise—she's watched countless videos about it—but she feels too tired, too overwhelmed, too... stuck.

She opens her phone again. Checks her email. Checks her texts. Checks Instagram. Checks TikTok. The cycle continues.

Sarah isn't lazy. She isn't weak. She's drowning in a different kind of flood—not of information, but of instability. Her mind won't settle. Her emotions swing wildly. She can't focus on anything for more than minutes. She craves instant relief, instant validation, instant anything to quiet the chaos inside. And the more she seeks it, the worse it gets.

She's not alone.

Across the world, millions of people wake up feeling exactly like Sarah. Anxious without knowing why. Restless but unable to act. Lonely despite being constantly "connected." Craving stillness but addicted to stimulation. Knowing what they should do but sustaining it for barely a day or two before collapsing back into old patterns.

We live in an age of unprecedented mental health crisis. Depression rates are skyrocketing. Anxiety is epidemic. Loneliness—despite being more "connected" than ever—is at all-time highs. Our attention spans have shriveled. Our ability to be present with ourselves, let alone others, has atrophied. We reach for our phones a hundred times a day seeking comfort and find only temporary distraction.

We're not standing on solid ground anymore. We're floating, untethered, buffeted by every wind and wave. We have no center. No stability. No foundation.

And when you have no foundation, everything becomes exhausting. Every decision is overwhelming. Every challenge feels impossible. Every day is just... too much.

We need solid ground. We need something stable to stand on, something that doesn't shift with every mood, every notification, every comparison, every craving.

We need what the ancient world called Kurma – the tortoise who held up the world.

The Crisis of the Unstable Mind

The numbers tell part of the story: One in five adults experiences mental illness each year. Suicide rates have increased by 30% in the last two decades. Antidepressant use has surged. Therapy waitlists stretch for months. Among young people, the statistics are even more alarming—rates of depression and anxiety among teenagers have nearly doubled since 2010.

But statistics don't capture what it actually feels like.

It feels like waking up already tired. Like your mind is a browser with forty-seven tabs open, all of them buffering. Like you're simultaneously bored and overwhelmed. Like you know what you should do—eat better, sleep more, exercise, meditate, connect with people—but the gap between knowing and doing feels impossibly wide.

It feels like watching everyone else succeed on social media while you can't even get out of bed. Like needing constant stimulation because silence with your own thoughts is unbearable. Like every emotion is either numbness or too much. Like you're performing the role of "person who has it together" while internally you're barely holding on.

And underneath it all, there's a profound loneliness.

We have more ways to connect than ever before in human history. We can video call someone across the world. We can message a hundred people simultaneously. We can broadcast our lives to thousands of followers. And yet, we've never felt more alone.

Because connection—real connection—requires presence. It requires stillness. It requires the ability to be with someone, really be with them, without checking your phone, without thinking about the next thing, without performing for an invisible audience.

But we've lost that capacity. We're so fractured internally that we can't offer wholeness to anyone else. We're so distracted that we can't give attention. We're so unstable that we can't provide stability.

Sarah's 3 AM phone check isn't really about the likes. It's about the desperate need to feel anchored to something, anything. The validation of strangers becomes a substitute for actual connection because actual connection requires a self that is present and stable—and she doesn't feel like she has that anymore.

This is the instant gratification trap.

Our brains are wired for immediate feedback. Apps and platforms know this. Every swipe gives you something new. Every refresh might bring good news. Every notification triggers a small dopamine hit. It's designed to keep you coming back, not because it satisfies you, but because it doesn't—not fully, not for long.

So you check again. And again. And again.

And in the process, you lose your ability to do anything that doesn't provide instant reward. Reading a book? Too slow. Having a deep conversation? Too much effort. Sitting with uncomfortable feelings? Unbearable. Waiting for results from consistent effort? Impossible.

We want transformation now. Healing now. Peace now. Success now. And when it doesn't come immediately, we give up and scroll some more.

The cruel irony is that the things that would actually help—meditation, exercise, therapy, deep relationships, meaningful work—all require exactly what we've lost: the ability to stay with something even when it's difficult, even when the rewards aren't immediate, even when we don't feel like it.

They require a stable foundation. And we're building on sand.

We can navigate the information flood, as Matsya taught us. But if we're too mentally fractured to think clearly, if we're too lonely to trust anyone, if we're too addicted to instant gratification to follow through on anything, if we're too unstable to stand firm in our decisions—what good does navigation do?

We need more than a guide through the chaos. We need to become people who can stand steady in the storm.

We need what we've lost: a foundation that doesn't move.

The Tortoise Who Held the World

Long ago, the gods and demons faced a crisis.

The nectar of immortality—*amrut*—had been lost in the cosmic ocean. Without it, the gods would lose their power. The universe would fall into chaos. Everything would be destroyed.

To retrieve it, they needed to churn the ocean of milk, the way you might churn butter from cream. But this was no ordinary ocean. It was vast, primordial, containing all of creation's potential and all of its poisons. And churning it would require an effort beyond what any single being could accomplish.

So the gods and demons formed an unlikely alliance. They would work together, despite being enemies, because the alternative was annihilation for everyone.

For the churning rod, they used Mount Mandara—a mountain so massive it scraped the heavens. For the rope, they used Vasuki, the great serpent, wrapping him around the mountain. The gods held one end of the serpent. The demons held the other. And they began to pull, back and forth, turning the mountain, churning the ocean.

But immediately, there was a problem.

Mount Mandara had no foundation. The moment they began to churn, the mountain started to sink into the ocean's depths. Without a base, without something solid beneath it, all their effort was useless. The mountain was too heavy. The ocean was too deep. Everything was collapsing.

This is when Vishnu took the form of Kurma—a massive tortoise.

Kurma dove beneath the churning ocean, positioned himself at the bottom, and offered his shell as the foundation for Mount Mandara. The mountain settled onto Kurma's back. Steady now. Stable. Supported.

And the churning could continue.

It wasn't easy. The ocean roiled and boiled. Terrible things emerged first—poison so potent it could destroy all creation. Shiva had to drink it to save everyone, holding it in his throat where it turned him blue. Then came tribulations, tests, challenges. The churning went on for a thousand years.

But Kurma never moved. Never wavered. Never complained.

He simply held steady. Patient. Unshakable. Providing the one thing that made everything else possible: solid ground.

Eventually, the nectar of immortality emerged. The gods were saved. The universe was preserved. But none of it would have happened without Kurma. Without the foundation, all the effort of gods and demons together was worthless.

The tortoise didn't churn the ocean. He didn't fight the demons. He didn't drink the poison. He didn't claim the nectar.

He did something more fundamental: he provided stability when Mandara was sinking.

And here's what's important to understand about Kurma's choice: he went down. While everyone else was focused upward—on getting the *amrut,* on winning, on achieving—Kurma went to the depths. He positioned himself at the bottom, in the darkness, beneath everything, unseen.

He became the foundation that no one would see but everyone would need.

There's a reason Vishnu chose a tortoise for this task and not something more impressive. Not an eagle. Not a lion. Not something fast or flashy or powerful in the ways we usually recognize.

A tortoise is slow. Deliberate. Patient. Steady. Able to withdraw into itself for protection. Able to carry great weight. Able to remain calm when everything around it is turbulent.

These aren't the qualities our world celebrates. We celebrate speed, intensity, constant motion, always being "on." We admire people who never stop, never slow down, never need rest.

But Kurma teaches something different: true power comes from stability. Real strength comes from the ability to remain steady when everything else is spinning out of control.

Without that foundation, nothing else works.

Building Your Foundation

Do you see yourself in this story?

You're trying to churn your own ocean. You're trying to extract something precious from the chaos of modern life—meaning, peace, success, connection, health. You're pulling hard. You're putting in effort. You're doing all the right things, or trying to.

But nothing's working. Not really. Not sustainably.

Because you're missing what Kurma provided: a foundation.

Without internal stability, all your effort just makes you sink deeper. You try to meditate, but you can't sit still. You try to build relationships, but you're too distracted to be present. You try to pursue meaningful work, but you can't focus long enough to make progress. You try to break bad habits, but the moment things get difficult, you collapse back into them.

It's not that you're not trying hard enough. It's that you're trying to churn the ocean while Mount Mandara is sinking into the depths.

You need to become Kurma in your own life. You need to go down, go inward, and build something solid at the bottom before you can achieve anything meaningful at the top.

This is the opposite of what our culture tells us to do.

Our culture says: Go faster. Do more. Optimize everything. Hack your productivity. Maximize your potential. Never stop. Never slow down. If you're not constantly achieving, constantly improving, constantly moving, you're failing.

But Kurma says: Slow down. Go deeper. Be still. Provide yourself with the stability that makes everything else possible.

Sarah, checking her phone at 3 AM, doesn't need another productivity hack. She doesn't need to optimize her morning routine or find a better time management system. She needs to stop sinking. She needs solid ground beneath her feet.

She needs to become the tortoise.

What does this actually mean?

It means recognizing that internal stability isn't a luxury—it's the foundation for everything else. It means understanding that the work of going inward, of building mental and emotional resilience, of learning to regulate your own nervous system—this isn't selfish or indulgent. It's essential.

Just like Kurma had to position himself at the bottom, unseen, doing work that looked like nothing from the outside but made everything else possible—you have to do the internal work that no one sees, that doesn't show up on Instagram, that doesn't impress anyone, but that makes your life actually work.

This requires three things that Kurma embodied: patience, steadiness, and the willingness to go beneath.

First, patience

Kurma held the mountain for a thousand years. He didn't demand quick results. He didn't give up when things got difficult. He understood that some things—important things—take time.

Building real mental and emotional stability is like this. It's not a weekend workshop. It's not a 30-day challenge. It's not something you hack or optimize your way into.

It's slow, unglamorous work. Daily meditation practice that feels boring. Regular therapy that sometimes seems like it's not helping. Exercise that doesn't give you abs in a week. Sleep routines that require saying no to things you want to do. Relationships that take years to deepen.

Our instant-gratification culture has made us allergic to this kind of patience. We want transformation now. We want to feel better immediately. And when we don't, we quit and try the next thing.

But stability doesn't work that way. The tortoise doesn't rush. And neither can you, if you want a foundation that actually holds.

Second, steadiness

The ocean churned violently around Kurma. Poison emerged. Demons and Gods fought. Everything was turbulent. But Kurma remained steady.

This is what you're building toward: the ability to remain calm in your own center even when everything around you—and inside you—is chaotic.

When the anxiety comes, you don't collapse into it or run from it. You feel it, acknowledge it, and remain steady. When the urge to check your phone hits, you notice it without immediately obeying it. When someone's success triggers your insecurity, you can sit with that feeling without letting it destroy you.

This isn't about never feeling difficult emotions. It's about having a stable core that doesn't get washed away by every wave.

Sarah's problem isn't that she feels anxious—it's that she has no stability beneath the anxiety. So every anxious thought sends her spiraling.

Every trigger knocks her completely off balance. She's at the mercy of every mood, every notification, every comparison.

Kurma teaches her: build something in yourself that doesn't move, even when everything else does.

Third, the willingness to go beneath

This is perhaps the hardest part. Kurma went down. He went to the depths, to the darkness, to the place no one could see.

For you, this means being willing to go inward, to face what you've been avoiding, to sit with the discomfort you've been distracting yourself from.

Why do you reach for your phone constantly? What are you trying not to feel? Why can't you be alone with your thoughts? What's underneath the anxiety? Why do you need constant validation? What wound are you trying to heal with likes and follows?

These are hard questions. It's easier to stay on the surface, to keep churning, to keep trying to achieve your way out of the discomfort.

But real stability requires going down to the foundation and doing the repair work there. It requires therapy, or journaling, or meditation, or whatever practice helps you honestly examine what's beneath your patterns.

It's work no one will see. No one will praise you for it. It won't make a good Instagram post. But it's the work that makes everything else possible.

What Kurma Would Do Today

So how do you actually become the tortoise? How do you build a foundation when you feel like you're already drowning?

Here are practices inspired by the avatar who held up the world:

Start with the body, not the mind

Kurma was physical. A body. A shell. Solid matter providing support.

When you're mentally unstable, trying to fix it with your mind alone is like trying to lift yourself by your own hair. Your thoughts are part of the problem—they're racing, spiraling, unreliable.

Start with your body instead.

This means: regulate your nervous system first. Your brain follows your body more than you realize. When your body is in fight-or-flight mode constantly—heart racing, breath shallow, muscles tense—your mind will be chaotic no matter how much you try to think your way out of it.

Learn to breathe deeply. Literally. Right now, take a breath that fills your belly, not just your chest. Hold it for four counts. Release slowly for six counts. Do this five times when you notice anxiety rising.

Move your body every day. Not to look good or burn calories—to discharge the stress hormones that keep you wired. Walk. Dance. Stretch. Anything that gets you out of your head and into your physical self.

Sleep like it's your job. Because it is. Sleep deprivation makes everything harder—regulating emotions, focusing, resisting impulses. Protect your sleep the way Kurma protected the foundation. No phone in bed. Consistent sleep time. Dark room. Whatever it takes.

Create non-negotiable anchors

Kurma didn't move. That was his whole purpose. He was the thing that stayed constant.

You need constants in your life too—practices that happen no matter what, that don't depend on motivation or mood or whether you feel like it.

Not ten things. Not a complex routine you'll abandon in a week. One or two non-negotiable anchors.

Maybe it's ten minutes of meditation every morning. Not when you feel like it. Not when you have time. Every morning, period. Even if it's uncomfortable. Especially if it's uncomfortable. The discomfort is where stability is built.

Maybe it's a weekly dance class. Non-negotiable. Even when you think you don't want to that week. Even when it's inconvenient. Consistency is the point.

Maybe it's a daily walk. Same time. Same commitment. Whether it's raining or sunny, whether you're busy or free.

The specific practice matters less than the consistency. Kurma's power wasn't in what he did—he just sat there. It was in the fact that he never wavered.

Your non-negotiable anchor becomes the foundation everything else is built on. It's the one thing you can count on when everything else is chaos. It's proof to yourself that you can be steady even when you don't feel steady.

Practice the pause between stimulus and response

The tortoise is slow. It doesn't react instantly to everything. There's a gap—a sacred pause—between what happens and how it responds.

You need to rebuild this capacity. Modern life has trained you to react instantly. Notification? Check immediately. Feeling? Escape immediately. Urge? Satisfy immediately.

But between every stimulus and your response, there's a space. And in that space lives your freedom.

Start small. When your phone buzzes, don't grab it immediately. Wait. Count to ten. Notice the urge without obeying it. Then, consciously decide whether to check it.

When someone says something that triggers you, don't fire back instantly. Breathe. Feel the emotion. Let it exist for five seconds before you respond.

When you have the urge to scroll, to eat, to buy something, to do anything compulsive—pause. Not forever. Just pause. Notice what you're feeling. Ask yourself what you actually need in this moment.

This is how you build the gap between your impulses and your actions. This is how you stop being at the mercy of every craving, every trigger, every mood. This is how you become stable instead of reactive.

Withdraw when necessary

The tortoise has a shell. When things get dangerous, it pulls inside. This isn't weakness—it's wisdom.

You're allowed to withdraw. You're allowed to protect your peace. You're allowed to say no to things that destabilize you, even if other people don't understand.

Maybe this means deleting social media apps for a month. Maybe it means saying no to social obligations when you're already stretched thin. Maybe it means setting boundaries with people who consistently leave you drained. Maybe it means turning off the news when it's making you spiral.

This isn't about hiding from life. It's about recognizing that you can't be a stable foundation for anything—not your work, not your relationships, not your goals—if you're constantly being battered by forces that destabilize you.

Kurma withdrew to the depths, away from the surface chaos. Sometimes you need to do the same. Create space. Get quiet. Protect yourself while you're building strength.

Commit to one thing deeply, not many things shallowly

The gods and demons were pulling in opposite directions. Everything was turbulent, contradictory, chaotic. Kurma's power was that he had one job and he did it completely.

You're probably trying to do too many things. Improve your career, your relationships, your health, your finances, your personal growth, your social life—all at once, all right now. And you're doing all of them shallowly because you're spread too thin.

Choose one foundation to build first. Just one.

Maybe it's mental health—getting therapy, building a meditation practice, learning to regulate your emotions. Maybe it's physical health—consistent sleep, regular movement, proper nutrition. Maybe it's one key relationship that needs depth. Maybe it's one skill you're developing.

Not five things. One.

Go deep with it. Be patient with it. Stay with it even when it's hard, even when you're not seeing results yet, even when something else seems more exciting.

This is countercultural. We're told to optimize everything simultaneously. But Kurma teaches us that depth creates stability, not breadth. One thing done completely is worth more than ten things done halfway.

Build your community of stability

Kurma didn't churn the ocean alone—but he also didn't try to do everyone else's job. The gods and demons had their roles. Kurma had his. Together, they accomplished what none could do alone.

You need people around you who value stability too. Not people who glorify the hustle. Not people who shame you for resting. Not people who make you feel bad for having boundaries or saying no or prioritizing your mental health.

Find the people who understand that building a foundation is work. Who respect your non-negotiables. Who support your withdrawal when you need it. Who are doing their own internal work and can walk alongside you in yours.

This might mean changing who you spend time with. It might mean being more selective about whose advice you take. It might mean joining a meditation group, or a support group, or finding a book club, or cultivating friendships with people who are also trying to live more intentionally.

You become like the people you surround yourself with. If everyone around you is frantic, chaotic, and unstable, you will be too. If you're surrounded by people who value steadiness, you'll find it easier to be steady yourself.

What Kurma Cannot Do

But, this is what we need to understand: even with perfect internal stability, even if you built an unshakeable foundation, even if you became as steady as the tortoise himself—you would still face crises that stability alone cannot solve.

Because the world isn't just chaotic inside your head. It's genuinely broken outside of it.

You can meditate every morning. You can regulate your nervous system perfectly. You can be completely present and stable and grounded. And then you'll turn on the news and see authoritarians dismantling democracy. You'll see the planet burning. You'll see corruption so deep in our institutions that trust itself seems naive. You'll see people's egos and greed causing real harm to real people.

Kurma can help you not fall apart when you see these things. But he can't fix them.

Think about it: Sarah can build all the internal stability in the world. She can learn to sleep through the night, to be present with her feelings, to resist the pull of her phone. And that's crucial—without it, she's useless to herself and everyone else.

But then what?

Her stability doesn't stop the systems that exploit her attention for profit. It doesn't challenge the authoritarians who benefit from her distraction. It doesn't heal the environmental destruction that her children will inherit. It doesn't address the corruption in institutions that eroded trust in the first place. It doesn't humble the narcissists in power who create chaos for personal gain.

Internal work is necessary. But it's not sufficient.

The dangerous thing about the self-help movement, about all the focus on personal growth and inner peace, is that it can become a way of avoiding the outer work. You can become so focused on your own healing that you ignore the fact that the world needs healing too.

This is the uncomfortable truth: building your foundation is essential, but it's also just the beginning.

The world needs you stable enough to act. Not stable instead of acting.

You have to do this work first. You have to build your foundation. You have to become steady. Because if you try to change the world while you're falling apart inside, you'll either burn out or become part of the problem.

But once you're stable?

Then you're dangerous to everything that depends on your chaos.

Then you can see clearly enough to discern truth from lies, thanks to Matsya. And you can stand firmly enough to act on what you see, thanks to Kurma.

But action itself? Confronting evil? Protecting what matters? Transforming broken systems?

That requires the other avatars.

The foundation is built. Now the real work begins.

* * *

3

Varaha - Rescuing What's Drowning

David stands in his backyard, staring at the brown grass.

It's been the hottest summer on record—again. The third year in a row. His lawn, which he's watered religiously despite the drought warnings, looks dead anyway. The oak tree his grandfather planted fifty years ago has started dropping leaves in July. The bird feeder he hung last spring sits untouched. He hasn't heard birds in weeks.

He pulls out his phone and checks the air quality index. Code Orange. Unhealthy for sensitive groups. There are wildfires three hundred miles away, but the smoke has turned the sky a sickly yellow. His daughter's school canceled outdoor recess again.

David goes back inside, into the air conditioning. He closes the blinds against the heat and the ugly sky. He'll order dinner tonight—no point heating up the kitchen. Everything will come in plastic containers that he'll throw away because the recycling program was cut due to budget constraints, and anyway, he read somewhere that most of it ends up in the ocean regardless.

His daughter, Emily, is on her iPad. She's watching videos of pristine beaches and coral reefs—places that look nothing like the actual beach they visited last month, which was covered in trash and smelled like dead fish.

"Dad, what's climate change?" she asks, not looking up from the screen.

David's stomach tightens. He's been dreading this question. How do you explain to a seven-year-old that the adults broke the world? That by the time she's his age, summers might be uninhabitable? That the animals she loves might not exist anymore? That the forests are burning, the ice is melting, the oceans are rising, and nobody seems to be doing nearly enough to stop it?

"It's... complicated, honey," he says.

She goes back to her video. A turtle swimming through clear blue water. David knows that turtle is probably swimming through a garbage patch now, if it's still alive at all.

He used to love nature. As a kid, he spent entire summers outside—climbing trees, catching frogs, building forts in the woods. He knew the names of birds and plants. He felt connected to something larger than himself.

Now? He sees nature as something happening on screens. Something distant. Something abstract. Something dying, and he doesn't know how to save it or even if it can be saved.

He goes to his laptop and scrolls past another article about carbon emissions. Another report about species extinction. Another prediction about how bad things will get. The numbers are so large they've stopped meaning anything. 1.5 degrees. 2 degrees. Six feet of sea level rise. One million species at risk.

He closes the laptop. Orders dinner. Throws away the containers. Turns up the air conditioning.

And feels absolutely powerless.

David isn't a bad person. He recycles when he can. He's thought about getting an electric car. He's donated to environmental organizations. But the problem feels so massive, so overwhelming, so far beyond what any individual can address, that he's stopped trying in any meaningful way.

And underneath his helplessness is something deeper: he's lost his connection to the Earth itself. He doesn't feel part of nature anymore. He feels separate from it, protected from it by his house and his car and his screens. Nature is something he sees through windows, not something he's embedded in.

The planet is drowning. And we've forgotten how to swim.

Across the world, millions of people feel exactly like David. We watch the environmental crisis unfold like a slow-motion apocalypse. We see the reports, the warnings, the disasters. We feel guilty, anxious, overwhelmed. We make small gestures that feel meaningless against the scale of the problem.

And we've become so disconnected from the natural world that we don't even fully grasp what we're losing. We live in climate-controlled boxes, commute in climate-controlled vehicles, work in climate-controlled buildings. We see trees as decoration, not as living beings we depend on. We think of "the environment" as something separate from us, something "out there," not the very foundation of our existence.

The Earth is being dragged into the depths. And most of us are too disconnected to even feel it happening.

We need what the ancient world called Varaha.

The boar who rescued the Earth from drowning.

The Drowning Planet

The statistics are numbing in their enormity.

Global temperatures have risen 1.2 degrees Celsius since pre-industrial times, and we're on track for 2.5 to 3 degrees by century's end. The last decade was the hottest on record. Ice sheets are melting faster than predicted. Sea levels are rising. Extreme weather events—hurricanes, floods, droughts, wildfires—are becoming more frequent and more severe.

We've lost 40% of wildlife populations since 1970. Species are going extinct at rates not seen since the dinosaurs disappeared. Coral reefs are bleaching and dying. Forests are burning or being cut down. Ocean acidification is killing marine ecosystems. Plastic has infiltrated every corner of the planet, from the deepest ocean trenches to the highest mountain peaks to the bodies of newborn babies.

The air in major cities is often too polluted to breathe safely. Water sources are contaminated or depleting. Soil is eroding. Pollinators are vanishing. The intricate web of life that took billions of years to evolve is unraveling in real time.

It feels like watching something precious die slowly while everyone pretends it's fine. Like being told your house is on fire but you should just keep calm and carry on. Like screaming into a void while the adults in charge argue about whether the void exists.

It feels like grief that has no outlet because the loss is ongoing, never-ending, everywhere.

Environmental psychologists have a term for this: ecological grief. The distress caused by witnessing environmental destruction. The mourning for ecosystems that are dying, species that are vanishing, landscapes that are changing beyond recognition. The anticipatory grief for a future that looks increasingly catastrophic.

David feels it when he looks at his daughter and imagines what kind of world she'll inherit. Parents everywhere feel it—the guilt of bringing children into a world we're destroying, the helplessness of not being able to protect them from what's coming.

Young people feel it acutely. They're inheriting a crisis they didn't create, one that will define their entire lives. The anxiety, the anger, the despair—it's not irrationality. It's the only sane response to the trajectory we're on.

David lives in a world where nature is optional. He can go days, weeks, without touching soil, without seeing a wild animal, without hearing wind through trees. His food comes from stores, his water from taps, his air from filters. He's insulated from the natural world by layers of human-made systems.

This disconnection isn't accidental. It's the culmination of centuries of thinking that positioned humans as separate from and superior to nature. That treated the Earth as a resource to be exploited rather than a living system we're part of. That built cities and economies that divorced us from the rhythms of the natural world.

We've forgotten that we don't just live on the Earth. We are Earth. Our bodies are made of the same elements, organized by the same evolutionary processes, sustained by the same cycles. There is no separation. The boundary between "us" and "nature" is an illusion.

But when you live entirely within human-made environments, when your only contact with nature is through screens or carefully manicured parks, when you can go months without experiencing true wildness—you forget this. Nature becomes abstract. Theoretical. Something that exists in documentaries and vacation destinations.

And when nature becomes abstract, its destruction becomes abstract too.

The numbers stop meaning anything. A million species at risk? Our brains can't process that scale. Three degrees of warming? It's just a number. Ice sheets collapsing? They're far away, not our problem.

Consider how we talk about climate change. We debate it like it's a political issue, an economic issue, a technological issue. We argue about carbon taxes and renewable energy and whether individual actions matter. All of this is important, yes. But we're missing something fundamental.

This isn't just an environmental crisis. It's a spiritual crisis. A crisis of relationship. We've broken our bond with the Earth, and now the Earth is breaking.

David can't save his daughter from climate change by recycling more. The solution isn't better individual habits, though those matter. The solution is remembering—viscerally, undeniably—that he and Emily and everyone else are not separate from nature. They are nature. What happens to the forests happens to them. What happens to the oceans happens to them. The Earth isn't drowning apart from us. We're drowning with it.

And we can't rescue what we don't love. We can't fight for what we don't feel connected to. We can't summon the will to make the massive changes necessary—personally, politically, economically—if nature is just an abstraction, just statistics, just something happening somewhere else to someone else.

We need to fall back in love with the Earth. We need to remember what it feels like to be held by something larger than ourselves. We need to reconnect to the wild, to the rhythms, to the aliveness that surrounds us even in our human-made habitats.

We need to remember that we're not standing on the Earth. We're standing as Earth, in one of its infinite expressions.

And then, maybe, we'll have the courage and the will to do what Varaha did: dive into the depths and rescue what's drowning, no matter how impossible it seems.

The Boar Who Saved the Earth

Long ago, the Earth herself was in mortal danger.

A demon named Hiranyaksha—his name means "golden-eyed"—had grown drunk on his own power. He had conquered the heavens. He had defeated the gods. He had thrown the cosmic order into chaos.

But conquest wasn't enough for him. He wanted to prove his dominance over everything, even creation itself.

So he did the unthinkable: he seized the Earth—Bhudevi, the goddess who embodies the planet—and dragged her down into the cosmic ocean, into the primordial waters that existed before form, before life, before anything.

The Earth was drowning in the depths, hidden in darkness, suffocating under the weight of water and the grip of a demon who cared nothing for her survival.

The gods panicked. Without the Earth, there could be no life, no stability, no foundation for existence. Everything depended on her. But Hiranyaksha was too powerful. No one could defeat him. No one could descend to those depths and retrieve what he had stolen.

This is when Vishnu took the form of Varaha—a boar.

Not a beautiful form. Not a noble form. Not something elegant or impressive in the ways gods usually appear. A boar. An animal that roots in mud, that digs in dirt, that isn't afraid to get filthy in pursuit of what it needs.

Varaha dove into the cosmic ocean without hesitation. Down, down, down into the darkness, into the crushing pressure, into the depths where no light reached. He searched through the murky waters while the demon taunted him, while everything seemed hopeless, while the task seemed impossible.

And then he found her. The Earth, submerged, barely holding on.

Varaha used his tusks—designed for digging, for uprooting, for bringing what's buried back to the surface. He lifted the Earth onto his tusks, massive and steady, carrying the entire weight of the planet on his own body. And he began the slow, exhausting journey back up.

But Hiranyaksha wasn't done. The demon attacked Varaha in the depths, determined to keep his prize, to prevent the rescue. The battle was fierce and long—lasting, some say, for a thousand years. Blow after blow in the darkness of the cosmic ocean.

Varaha didn't give up. He held the Earth steady on his tusks even while fighting. He protected her even while being assaulted. He refused to drop his burden no matter how difficult the battle became.

Finally, Varaha killed Hiranyaksha. Not through trickery or diplomacy or appeals to reason. Through direct confrontation. Through the willingness to fight for what mattered, to use force when force was necessary, to destroy what was destroying creation.

And then, with the demon defeated, Varaha carried the Earth back to the surface. He placed her gently back in her rightful place. He restored her to stability, to the position where life could flourish again.

The Earth was saved. Not because someone negotiated with the demon. Not because someone wished really hard or hoped for the best or waited for someone else to handle it. But because someone was willing to dive into the depths, get dirty, fight fiercely, and carry the weight of the world.

Here's what's important about Varaha's form: he was a boar. An animal intimately connected to the earth—digging in soil, rooting for sustenance, comfortable in mud and mess. He wasn't afraid to get dirty. He understood that rescue work isn't clean or pretty or comfortable.

The boar doesn't mind getting its snout in the dirt. That's where the truth is, where the nourishment is, where the work happens. Varaha embodies this willingness to engage directly with the earth, with matter, with the messy physical reality of existence.

And his tusks—powerful, designed for uprooting and lifting—these weren't decorative. They were tools. Practical. Essential for the task. Varaha knew what he needed and he had it: the strength to lift what seemed unliftable, the tools to dig out what was buried, the determination to carry impossible weight.

The story also tells us something crucial: the Earth needed rescuing. She couldn't save herself from the depths. She needed someone to come for her, to fight for her, to lift her back up.

And the demon? Hiranyaksha represents more than just evil. He represents the force that drags the Earth down—greed, domination, the will to possess and exploit without care for consequences. He's the embodiment of treating the Earth as something to be conquered rather than something to be part of.

Varaha didn't reason with this force. He fought it. Because some things can't be negotiated with. Some forms of destruction have to be confronted directly and stopped by whatever means necessary.

The Earth was drowning. Varaha saved her. That's the story. Simple and profound.

And right now, in our world, the Earth is drowning again.

Becoming the Boar

Our Earth is drowning again. Not in a cosmic ocean, but under the weight of our extraction, our pollution, our exploitation, our disconnection. And we—humanity—are both Hiranyaksha and Varaha. We're both the demon dragging the Earth down and the potential savior who could rescue her.

The question is: which will we choose to be?

David, standing in his air-conditioned house, ordering plastic-wrapped dinner, feeling powerless—he's caught in the middle. He's not actively trying to destroy the planet, but he's also not diving in to save it. He's paralyzed. Disconnected. Waiting for someone else to be Varaha.

But that's not how this works.

Varaha didn't wait. He didn't form a committee to study the problem. He didn't debate whether rescuing the Earth was economically feasible or politically viable. He saw what needed to be done and he dove in.

This is what our moment requires. Not more analysis. Not more hand-wringing. Not more guilt without action. We need people willing to dive into the depths, get dirty, fight hard, and carry the weight.

What does Varaha teach us about rescuing the Earth?

He teaches us four essential things: reconnection, willingness to get dirty, fierce protection, and the strength to carry weight.

First, reconnection

Varaha was a boar—an animal of the earth. He wasn't separate from nature, observing it from a distance. He was nature. His entire being was designed for intimate contact with soil, with matter, with the physical world.

This is what we've lost and what we must reclaim.

David needs to stop experiencing nature through screens and start experiencing it through his body. Not as a tourist. Not as a spectator.

But as a participant, as someone who belongs to the Earth rather than someone who uses it.

This means: touch soil regularly. Not just once a year on vacation, but regularly. Garden, even if it's just herbs on a windowsill. Feel dirt on your hands. Understand that this—soil, earth, humus—is where everything comes from. Your food. Your body. Your life.

Walk barefoot on grass when you can. Feel the ground beneath you. Remember that you're standing on a living planet, not just a surface.

Learn the names of things. The trees in your neighborhood. The birds you hear. The plants that grow wild. When you know their names, they stop being "environment" and become neighbors, companions, kin.

Spend time outside without purpose, without productivity, without your phone. Just be present with the more-than-human world. Watch clouds. Listen to wind. Observe how light changes. These aren't luxuries. They're how you remember you're part of something larger.

Notice the seasons not on a calendar but in your body and in the world around you. When do specific birds arrive? When do certain flowers bloom? When does the quality of light shift? These rhythms are your rhythms—you evolved with them, through them.

The more you reconnect, the more you'll feel the crisis viscerally. And feeling it—really feeling it—is what transforms paralysis into action.

Second, willingness to get dirty

Varaha didn't maintain his dignity. He didn't stay clean and comfortable. He dove into the murky depths, into the mess, into the difficult and uncomfortable work.

Environmental action isn't pretty. It's not Instagram-worthy. It's messy, hard, often unglamorous work.

It means making uncomfortable changes. Giving up conveniences you've grown used to. Having difficult conversations with family and friends who don't want to hear it. Confronting systems that benefit you even as they harm the planet. Admitting your own complicity.

David drives a gas car. He eats meat. He lives in a house that's too big and climate-controlled to an absurd degree. He participates in a consumer economy that's destroying the Earth. Acknowledging this—really acknowledging it, not just feeling vaguely guilty—is uncomfortable. It's dirty work.

But that's where change begins. Not in the easy stuff. In the uncomfortable confrontation with how we actually live and what it actually costs.

Varaha teaches us that rescue work means being willing to root around in the dirt, to engage directly with the messy reality of what needs to change.

Third, fierce protection

Here's what many people miss about Varaha's story: he didn't just rescue the Earth. He fought for her. He killed the demon who was destroying her.

This is uncomfortable for us. We want to believe that environmental problems can be solved through education, through market forces, through gentle persuasion. Sometimes they can. But sometimes they can't.

Sometimes there are forces—corporations, governments, individuals—that profit from destruction and will not stop voluntarily. Sometimes the demon of exploitation has to be confronted directly.

This doesn't necessarily mean violence. But it does mean being willing to fight. To protest. To disrupt business-as-usual. To use whatever legal and ethical means necessary to stop the destruction.

It means divesting from industries that destroy the planet. Boycotting companies that refuse to change. Demanding accountability from those in power. Voting out politicians who prioritize profit over survival. Supporting litigation against environmental criminals.

David feels powerless partly because he's been taught that being a good citizen means being polite, not making waves, trusting that the adults in charge will handle things. But the adults in charge are failing catastrophically.

Varaha teaches us that sometimes protection requires confrontation. That sometimes you have to say "no" fiercely and mean it. That sometimes you have to stand in the way of destruction, even when it's costly, even when it's uncomfortable.

Fourth, the strength to carry weight

The most striking image in Varaha's story is him carrying the entire Earth on his tusks. The whole planet. All of it. The weight was immense, and he carried it.

This is perhaps the hardest teaching: that rescuing the Earth requires bearing weight that feels unbearable.

The weight of knowing. The weight of caring. The weight of responsibility. The weight of grief. The weight of action. The weight of persistence even when results seem impossibly distant.

David feels this weight and wants to put it down. It's too much. The problem is too big. What can one person do?

But Varaha didn't ask if the weight was too much. He lifted it anyway.

This doesn't mean any individual has to carry the whole burden alone—that would be impossible and unhealthy. But it does mean accepting your portion of the weight. Not avoiding it. Not pretending it isn't there. Not waiting for others to carry it for you.

It means living with the discomfort of knowing what's happening and choosing to act anyway, even when action feels futile. It means tolerating the emotional weight of caring about something that's being destroyed. It means accepting that you are a part of this crisis and therefore responsible for being part of the solution.

The weight doesn't get lighter by ignoring it. It gets lighter by sharing it—by finding others who will carry their portion too, by building movements where the burden is distributed.

But first, you have to be willing to pick it up.

What Varaha Would Do Today

So what does it actually look like to be Varaha in your own life? How do you dive in and start rescuing the Earth from drowning?

Here are practices inspired by the boar who saved the world:

Master the art of waste

Varaha knew how to dig, how to sort through matter, how to distinguish what's valuable from what's not. You need this same discernment with what you throw away.

Recycle properly. Learn what your local system accepts and follow those rules. Rinse containers before recycling—contaminated items ruin entire batches. When in doubt, research it or throw it in the trash. Bad recycling is worse than no recycling.

But here's the truth Varaha would tell you: recycling is the last resort, not the solution. The real work is reducing and reusing.

Refuse single-use everything

Varaha carried the Earth on his tusks because someone had to. You can refuse to add to the burden she's already carrying.

Keep reusable bags everywhere—in your car, by your door, in your backpack. It takes one week to build this habit. Say no to plastic straws, plastic utensils, unnecessary packaging. Bring your own containers when possible. Buy a reusable water bottle and actually use it.

Every piece of plastic you refuse is one piece that won't spend centuries breaking down into microplastics in the ocean.

This isn't about perfection. David will forget his bags sometimes. That's fine. What matters is the pattern, the consistent choice to refuse what's unnecessary.

Compost organic waste

Food scraps aren't garbage. They're potential soil. They're Earth waiting to become Earth again.

Start composting—whether in your yard, on your balcony, or through community programs. Coffee grounds, fruit and vegetable scraps, yard trimmings—all of this becomes rich soil instead of rotting in landfills and producing methane.

If you have outdoor space, compost there. If you don't, find local composting options or start small with indoor systems. The details don't matter as much as the commitment to returning organic matter to the earth.

Protect water and air

What goes down your drain ends up in waterways. Use environmentally-safe cleaning products. Dispose of medications properly—never flush them. Fix leaks. Use water consciously.

For air quality: drive less. Maintain your vehicle. Consider electric or hybrid when replacing your car. Plant trees wherever you can. Use less energy—turn off lights, unplug devices, adjust your thermostat. Support clean energy if it's available in your area.

These aren't glamorous actions, but they reduce the harm we cause to the systems that keep us alive.

Eat consciously

Industrial meat production is devastating for the planet—deforestation, emissions, water pollution, species extinction.

Start with meatless days each week. Buy local and seasonal when possible. Reduce food waste by planning meals and using leftovers. Grow some of your own food if you can, even if it's just herbs on a windowsill.

You're not just feeding yourself. You're voting with every meal for the kind of agriculture you want to exist.

Use your purchasing power wisely

Every bit of money you spend is a vote for the kind of world you want. Buy less overall. Use what you have longer. Repair instead of replace.

When you do buy, support businesses with genuine environmental commitments. Boycott those that refuse to change despite knowing the harm they cause.

Support policies and politicians who prioritize the planet. Vote in every election. Make your voice heard. The system responds to pressure when that pressure is consistent and loud.

Measure impact, not perfection

You will fail at this sometimes. You'll forget your bags. You'll make choices that harm the planet because the alternative was too difficult that day.

That's okay. The Earth doesn't need a few people doing environmentalism perfectly. It needs millions of people doing it imperfectly but consistently.

Track your progress. Celebrate improvements. David switching to meatless days? That matters. Reducing his trash by half? That's significant. Over time, these changes add up to real impact.

Be Varaha. Dive in. Get your hands dirty. Fight when necessary. Carry your portion of the weight.

The Earth is drowning. And you—yes, you—can help pull her back to the surface.

What Varaha Cannot Do

While our individual efforts being a Varaha can prove pivotal in rescuing the Earth, there is a broader issue that needs to be fixed to resolve the crisis.

Because individual action, while essential, isn't sufficient to rescue a drowning planet.

The environmental crisis isn't just the result of billions of individual bad choices. It's the result of systems designed to extract, exploit, and externalize costs. It's the result of corporations that have known about climate change for decades and chose profit over survival. It's the result of governments that prioritize economic growth over ecological stability. It's the result of an entire civilization built on the assumption that infinite growth on a finite planet is possible.

Varaha can teach you to reconnect with the Earth, to take responsibility for your impact, to do the practical work of reducing harm. But he can't dismantle the systems that make harmful choices the easiest and often the only affordable option.

Think about David. He can start composting, refuse plastic bags, eat less meat, drive less. And he should—these actions matter. But his individual choices don't stop oil companies from drilling. They don't prevent governments from subsidizing fossil fuels. They don't challenge the economic system that demands endless consumption. They don't hold accountable the corporations responsible for the vast majority of emissions.

David can reconnect with nature in his backyard while corporations clear-cut old-growth forests on the other side of the world. He can reduce his water use while industrial agriculture depletes aquifers. He can bike to work while his government approves new coal plants.

The demon Hiranyaksha wasn't defeated by individual good choices. He was defeated by direct confrontation, by someone willing to fight.

And here's where Varaha's limitations become clear: he rescued the Earth, yes. But he didn't transform the system that allowed the Earth to be dragged down in the first place. He didn't address the greed, the corruption, the authoritarian impulses, the massive egos that create and perpetuate environmental destruction.

You can be perfectly connected to nature and still live under leaders who deny climate science and dismantle environmental protections. You can carry the weight of ecological grief while authoritarians silence scientists and activists. You can do all the right things individually while corrupt institutions prioritize profit over survival.

Varaha gives you the foundation—the reconnection, the practical habits, the willingness to get dirty and carry weight. Without this, you're useless. You can't fight for the Earth if you don't feel part of it. You can't sustain activism if you haven't built the practices that keep you grounded.

But once you have that foundation?

Then you need Narasimha's fierce courage to confront the tyrants who are destroying the planet for power and profit. You need Vamana's humility to counter the massive egos—both corporate and individual—that refuse to acknowledge limits. You need Parashurama's righteous anger to dismantle the corrupt institutions that make environmental destruction profitable. You need Rama's ethics to navigate the compromises you'll be asked to make. You need Krishna's wisdom for the complex political and economic choices that have no easy answers.

Varaha rescued the Earth from the depths. But the demon of exploitation is still alive, still powerful, still dragging the planet down in new ways every day.

Individual responsibility is necessary. But it's not sufficient. Reconnection is essential. But it's not enough.

The Earth needs you connected to her, yes. But she also needs you willing to fight for her at every level—personal, political, systemic.

The boar dove deep and carried the Earth back to the surface. Now the question is: what kind of world will we build on that surface? One that respects limits and lives in balance? Or one that allows the same forces to drag her down again?

That requires every avatar. Working together. Starting with your own reconnection, but not ending there.

Never ending there.

* * *

4

Narasimha - When Evil Hides Behind the Rules

Priya sits in the staff meeting, her hands clenched under the table.

Her boss, Mr. Sharma, is speaking. Again. He's been speaking for forty minutes about "accountability" and "performance standards," but everyone in the room knows what this is really about. It's about Rahul, who reported Sharma for taking credit for his work. Rahul, who went to HR three weeks ago with documentation, with emails, with proof.

Rahul isn't at this meeting. He was "let go" yesterday. "Performance issues," the official email said. No one believes it. Everyone knows the truth. But no one says anything.

"I want to be clear," Sharma continues, his voice pleasant, almost friendly. "This company values transparency. My door is always open. But we also value loyalty. We're a family here. And families don't air their dirty laundry publicly."

The threat is clear even though he never says it directly. Speak up, and you'll be next.

Priya thinks about her mortgage. Her daughter's school fees. Her mother's medical bills. She thinks about how hard it was to get this job, how few opportunities there are for women her age in her field. She thinks about Rahul's empty desk.

She stays silent.

After the meeting, Sharma stops her in the hallway. "Priya, you've been doing excellent work. I'm considering you for the promotion to senior manager." He smiles. "I value team players. People who understand how things work here."

She knows what he's saying. Play along, benefit. Resist, suffer.

"Thank you, sir," she hears herself say.

She hates herself for it.

This is how tyranny works in the modern world. Not with obvious cruelty—though that exists too. But with a smile and carefully worded policies and the knowledge that the system protects those in power while punishing those who challenge them.

Sharma hasn't technically broken any laws. He's careful about that. He knows how to work within the rules, how to use policies meant to protect employees as weapons against them. How to retaliate without leaving evidence. How to make victims look like troublemakers. How to position himself as the reasonable one while destroying anyone who threatens his control.

He's not the CEO. He's not even that high up. But in his small sphere of power, he's untouchable. HR won't act—they already showed that. His boss won't question him—Sharma delivers results. The people beneath him won't unite—they're too afraid, too divided, too focused on survival.

This is tyranny at the micro level. And it exists everywhere.

In workplaces where bosses abuse power knowing HR serves management, not justice. In relationships where one partner controls through intimidation disguised as "love" or "protection." In communities where those with authority use it to silence, exploit, or harm with impunity. In governments where leaders bend rules they claim to uphold, punish dissent while praising democracy, and consolidate power while speaking of freedom.

The tyrants of our age rarely announce themselves as tyrants. They don't wear crowns or claim divine right. They operate within systems, using those systems' own rules and structures as weapons. They position themselves as legitimate, as following procedure, as maintaining order.

And the victims? They're made to look like troublemakers, complainers, threats to stability. The system protects the abuser while isolating the abused.

This is the crisis Narasimha confronted: power that has made itself invulnerable through the very structures meant to constrain it. Evil that hides behind legitimacy. Tyranny that cannot be defeated by following the rules because the tyrant controls the rules.

Priya goes back to her desk. Opens her laptop. Starts working. Says nothing.

And in her silence, the tyranny wins again.

Across the world, millions of people face versions of this. Authoritarian governments that call themselves democracies. Leaders who dismantle institutions while claiming to strengthen them. Systems of power that protect abusers—in families, workplaces, governments, communities. The helplessness of watching injustice unfold while being told the proper channels will handle it, knowing they won't.

We've learned to navigate information floods, as Matsya taught us. We've built internal stability, as Kurma showed us. We've reconnected with the Earth, as Varaha demanded. But what good is any of that if we live under power that crushes those who speak truth, who stand up, who resist?

We need what the ancient world called Narasimha.

The man-lion who tore apart a demon king who seemed impossible to defeat.

The Age of Hidden Tyranny

We think we've moved beyond tyranny. We have constitutions, laws, human rights declarations, democratic institutions. We believe the age of absolute power is over, that checks and balances protect us.

But abuse of power hasn't disappeared. It's evolved.

The reality is more nuanced than saying power always corrupts. Most people in positions of authority use that authority responsibly. Most leaders, managers, parents, teachers, officials—they're trying their best, operating in good faith, constrained by the same systems and pressures as everyone else.

But some don't. And when they don't, the damage is immense.

What makes modern abuse of power so destructive is how it hides. The tyrants of today rarely announce themselves as tyrants. They don't wear crowns or demand worship. They operate within systems, often using those systems' own rules as shields. They position themselves as legitimate, as following proper procedure, as maintaining necessary order.

The abuser of power today is often charming, articulate, and careful. They know how to position themselves as the victim when challenged. They know how to make their abuse look like discipline, their control look like leadership, their cruelty look like tough but necessary decisions.

And they have something their predecessors didn't: sophisticated systems of control that make resistance incredibly difficult.

Consider how this works in practice.

An authoritarian government doesn't need to ban all media—just control enough of it and discredit the rest as "fake news" or "enemies of the people." They don't need to arrest all dissidents—just arrest enough, publicly enough, to make everyone else self-censor out of fear.

A toxic boss doesn't need to fire everyone who questions them—just fire one person publicly, strategically, so everyone else gets the message. Create an environment where people police themselves, where fear does the work of control.

An abusive partner doesn't need to be violent every day—just often enough, unpredictably enough, that their victim is always on edge, always calculating, always trying to avoid the next explosion.

This is tyranny's genius: making people complicit in their own oppression. Making them choose silence. Making them believe resistance is futile or dangerous or not worth the cost.

Consider how this manifests across different contexts.

In some governments, we see democratic backsliding—leaders who restrict press freedom, undermine judicial independence, criminalize dissent, all while maintaining the appearance of democratic process. They don't abolish democracy; they hollow it out from within, keeping the shell while removing the substance.

In workplaces, there are managers who abuse their position—taking credit for others' work, retaliating against those who speak up, creating environments of fear while maintaining plausible deniability. When someone like Rahul reports misconduct with documentation, with proof, the system somehow protects the powerful while punishing the truthful.

In families, abuse often hides behind closed doors. One person controls through fear, manipulation, or violence, while the outside world sees a normal, functional household. Victims who speak up are often disbelieved or told they're exaggerating. "He seems so nice," people say. "She wouldn't do that."

In institutions—schools, hospitals, religious organizations—those with authority sometimes exploit it. A teacher who targets certain students. A doctor who dismisses patient concerns. A religious leader who uses spiritual authority for personal gain. And when victims come forward, they often face more scrutiny than the perpetrators.

What these situations share is a common pattern: power has positioned itself in ways that make accountability nearly impossible.

The abuser knows how to work the system. They know how to make their actions look defensible, their victims look unreasonable. They know how to use procedures meant to ensure fairness as weapons against those they harm. They know how to make retaliation look like legitimate consequence.

And this creates a terrible bind for those being harmed.

Priya faces this bind. She could report what she's witnessing. But she's seen how this plays out. The burden of proof falls on the victim. The process is long, exhausting, and often futile. Meanwhile, she has bills to pay, responsibilities she can't abandon, people depending on her.

So she stays silent. Not because she's weak, but because the cost of speaking up is calculated to be too high for most people to bear.

This is how abuse of power sustains itself in the modern age—not primarily through force, but by making resistance too costly, too isolated, too risky.

The proper channels exist, but they often serve to exhaust and discourage rather than deliver justice. Complaint processes that go nowhere. Appeals that take years. Procedures designed to protect the institution rather than address the wrong.

This creates a particular kind of despair. It's not the despair of facing open, obvious evil that everyone acknowledges. It's the despair of facing abuse that's protected, legitimized, defended by the very structures meant to prevent it.

We have clear information, thanks to Matsya. We have internal stability, thanks to Kurma. We have connection to what matters, thanks to Varaha. But when we face power that's made itself nearly invincible within systems, when we face abuse that hides behind legitimacy—what then?

Following procedures doesn't work when procedures protect the powerful. Being reasonable doesn't work when the unreasonable hold authority. Staying patient doesn't work when patience is weaponized as compliance.

But here's what abusers of power throughout history have always underestimated: there comes a point where silence becomes more unbearable than the cost of speaking. Where fear transforms into something stronger. Where enough people see clearly enough that the illusion of legitimacy shatters.

That's when abuse of power faces its greatest threat. Not from another authority, but from those who refuse to be silenced by the rules that protect the abuser.

This is what Narasimha represents. Not following the rules that make tyranny invincible. Not working within systems designed to protect abusers. But breaking through—fiercely, decisively, unstoppably—when breaking through is the only path to justice.

The Man-Lion Who Broke All Rules

Long ago, there was a demon king named Hiranyakashyap. His name meant "golden throne," and he wore his ambition openly. He wanted to be immortal, invincible, the supreme power in all creation.

He performed terrible austerities—meditating, fasting, standing on one leg for thousands of years—until he gained the attention of Brahma, the creator god himself.

Brahma appeared and offered him a boon.

Hiranyakashyap was clever. He didn't just ask for immortality—the gods would never grant that. Instead, he asked for something that seemed to make him functionally immortal through sheer specificity:

"Grant me that I cannot be killed by man or beast. Not indoors or outdoors. Not during day or night. Not on the ground or in the sky. Not by any weapon. Not by any god or demon or human."

Brahma granted it. How could he refuse? The request was specific, and specificity is a form of loophole, a way of working within cosmic rules.

And so Hiranyakashyap became invincible—or so he believed.

He conquered the three worlds. He dethroned gods. He demanded worship. Anyone who refused to acknowledge him as supreme faced torture or death. He made himself the law, the authority, the final word on everything.

And the worst part? He was technically within his rights. He had earned his boon through genuine austerity. He was using power he'd legitimately acquired. The rules of the cosmos protected him.

No one could touch him. No one could challenge him. The system he'd manipulated so carefully made him untouchable.

Except for one person who refused to comply: his own son, Prahlad.

Prahlad was devoted to Vishnu. Not out of rebellion, but out of genuine faith. He saw divinity as something beyond power, beyond kingship, beyond his father's tyranny. And no amount of torture, threats, or manipulation could make him worship Hiranyakashyap instead.

This drove the demon king to rage. His own son, defying him. His own child, undermining his authority.

Hiranyakashyap tried everything. He sent teachers to indoctrinate Prahlad. He had him thrown off cliffs, drowned, trampled by elephants, bitten by snakes—each time, Prahlad survived, protected by the divine force he believed in.

Finally, in a fit of fury, Hiranyakashyap confronted his son directly.

"If your god is everywhere, as you claim, is he in this pillar?" He struck a pillar in his throne room mockingly.

"Yes," Prahlad said simply. "He is."

"Then let him save you!" Hiranyakashyap raised his weapon to kill his own child.

And the pillar exploded.

From it emerged Narasimha—half man, half lion. Not man, not beast, but both. A form that existed in the space between categories, in the loophole of the loophole.

It was twilight—neither day nor night. Narasimha grabbed Hiranyakashyap and dragged him to the threshold of the palace—neither indoors nor outdoors. He placed the demon king on his lap—neither ground nor sky. And with his claws—not weapons—he tore Hiranyakashyap apart.

Every condition of the boon was technically fulfilled, yet all were circumvented. The system Hiranyakashyap had so carefully manipulated to make himself invincible became meaningless in the face of divine fury that refused to be constrained by those rules.

Narasimha didn't negotiate. Didn't appeal to higher authority. Didn't work within the system. He broke through it—literally, from a pillar—and destroyed what everyone said couldn't be destroyed.

And here's what's crucial: Narasimha was terrifying. Even after Hiranyakashyap was dead, Narasimha's rage didn't subside. The gods feared him. His fury was so immense, so absolute, that no one could approach him. Divine intervention had become divine wrath, and that wrath was nearly uncontrollable.

It was only Prahlad—the child, the victim, the one who had suffered under tyranny—who could approach Narasimha and calm him. Only innocence could gentle that fierce protector.

This tells us something important: the force required to break tyranny is necessarily fierce, possibly frightening, and must be handled carefully. Righteous anger is powerful and necessary, but it can consume everything if not tempered.

Narasimha represents the fury that rises when all other options have failed. When patience is exhausted. When following proper channels has proven futile. When the tyrant has made himself invincible through the very rules meant to constrain him.

Sometimes—not always, but sometimes—justice requires breaking the rules that protect injustice.

Sometimes the pillar must explode.

Becoming the Man-Lion

Priya knows this story. Not the details, maybe. Not the names or the cosmic ocean or the specific boons. But she knows the essential truth of it: power that makes itself untouchable through the very rules meant to constrain it. Evil that hides behind legitimacy. A system that protects the abuser while isolating the victim.

She lives inside this story every day.

Sharma is her Hiranyakashyap — not a demon king with cosmic power, but a middle manager with just enough authority to destroy the people beneath him while remaining protected by the structures above him. He's learned exactly which rules to follow and which to bend. He knows how to make his tyranny look like leadership, his retaliation look like performance management, his abuse look like necessary discipline.

And the system—HR, his superiors, company policy, legal protections for management—these are his boons. Not granted by gods, but built into the architecture of corporate power. They make him functionally invincible within his domain, just as Hiranyakashyap's conditions made him invincible within his.

The proper channels Priya is supposed to use? They're the very rules Sharma has learned to weaponize. Filing a complaint through HR is like trying to defeat Hiranyakashyap by following the exact conditions of his protection. It's playing a game where the tyrant wrote the rules.

What Narasimha understood—what Priya needs to understand—is that some systems are so corrupted by the power they're meant to constrain that working within them only strengthens the tyrant's grip.

The pillar had to explode. The rules had to be circumvented. The boons that made Hiranyakashyap invincible had to be rendered meaningless by approaching from an angle they didn't account for.

This doesn't mean abandon all structure or embrace chaos. It doesn't mean violence or cruelty or becoming what you're fighting against. Narasimha's fury was righteous, directed, purposeful—not random destruction but precise intervention at the exact point where evil thought itself safe.

What it means is this: when the system protects the abuser, you need to find ways to operate outside that system's control.

Narasimha teaches us four essential truths about confronting tyranny: refusing to play by rigged rules, righteous fury, strategic disruption, and knowing when the fight is over.

First, refusing to play by rigged rules

Hiranyakashyap had made himself invincible within the system. Every rule, every constraint, every boundary had been carefully navigated to protect him. Defeating him within those rules was impossible.

Narasimha didn't try. He came from the pillar—from outside the expected boundaries. He was neither man nor beast, operating in the space between categories that Hiranyakashyap's protections didn't account for.

For Priya, this means recognizing when the game is rigged and refusing to keep playing it the way Sharma expects.

She could spend years filing complaints through official channels, documenting everything, appealing decisions, following every procedure. And Sharma would use every one of those procedures against her. The process itself would exhaust her while protecting him.

But what if she refuses to play that game? What if she documents everything and takes it public? What if she finds others Sharma has harmed and they speak together instead of separately? What if she contacts the board directly, or the media, or regulatory bodies outside the company's control? What if she simply leaves and warns others publicly about what they're walking into?

These are the pillars exploding. These are the approaches from angles the tyrant didn't account for because they operate outside the system he controls.

This isn't about breaking laws or embracing chaos. It's about refusing to be constrained by processes designed to protect the powerful. It's about finding the spaces between the rules where justice can still operate.

Second, righteous fury

Narasimha wasn't calm. He wasn't measured. He was furious. His rage was absolute, terrifying, barely controllable.

We're taught to suppress anger, especially when confronting authority. Stay professional. Don't be emotional. Keep your cool. Be reasonable.

But fury—righteous fury at injustice—is appropriate. It's necessary. It's the energy that finally says "enough."

Priya's calm compliance is killing her. Her reasonable accommodation of unreasonable abuse is destroying her sense of self. Her professional demeanor in the face of injustice is enabling that injustice to continue.

She needs to get angry. Not petty, not vindictive, not destructive for its own sake. But righteously, clearly, powerfully angry at what's being done and what's being allowed.

This doesn't mean losing control. Narasimha's fury was directed, purposeful, and ultimately successful. But it was fury nonetheless—the fierce rejection of tyranny, the absolute refusal to accept injustice as inevitable.

Your anger at abuse of power isn't a character flaw. It's a moral response. It's what happens when you're connected enough to recognize wrong and stable enough to refuse to normalize it. Don't suppress it. Channel it.

Third, strategic disruption

Narasimha didn't fight Hiranyakashyap everywhere at once. He appeared at a specific moment—when the demon king was about to kill his own child. He targeted a specific vulnerability—the gap between all those careful conditions. He acted decisively, not gradually.

Confronting entrenched power requires strategy, not just courage. You can't fight tyranny on every front simultaneously. You have to identify where it's vulnerable and strike there.

For Priya, this might mean identifying exactly what Sharma cares about most—his reputation, his relationship with his superiors, his carefully constructed image—and threatening that specifically. It might mean timing her action for when he's most exposed—during a review period, when his boss is paying attention, when he's already under scrutiny for something else.

It means being smart, not just brave. It means understanding that righteous fury needs to be directed strategically, not scattered everywhere.

Disruption isn't chaos. It's the precise application of pressure at the point where the system can't absorb it without change.

Fourth, knowing when the fight is over

Here's what often gets forgotten about Narasimha's story: he had to be calmed. His fury, once unleashed, didn't automatically subside when Hiranyakashyap was dead. It took Prahlad—innocent, gentle Prahlad—to approach him and bring him back from that rage.

This is crucial. The fierce energy required to break tyranny can become tyrannical itself if not tempered. Righteous anger can become self-righteous cruelty. The drive to destroy abuse can become destructive for its own sake.

You need to know when the fight is over. When the tyrant is defeated, when the system has changed, when justice has been served—you need to be able to step back from the fury that got you there.

This is why movements against tyranny need both the fierce warriors and the gentle healers. Both the Narasimhas who break through and the Prahlads who know when to say "enough, it's done, we can rest now."

Priya will need this. If she confronts Sharma successfully, if she brings him down, if she changes the system—she'll need to resist the temptation to let victory become vindictiveness. To let justified anger become perpetual bitterness. To let the fight that was necessary consume her entire identity.

Fight fiercely. But know when to stop fighting.

What Narasimha Would Do Today

So what does it actually look like to be Narasimha in your own life? How do you confront abuse of power when the system protects the abuser?

Here are practices inspired by the man-lion who broke through the pillar:

Document everything—but know documentation isn't enough

Narasimha knew exactly what Hiranyakashyap had done. The facts were clear. But facts alone don't defeat tyrants—action does.

If you're facing abuse of power, document everything. Dates, times, witnesses, emails, messages, specific incidents. Keep records outside systems the abuser controls—personal email, cloud storage they can't access, physical copies at home.

But understand this: documentation proves you're right, but it doesn't automatically defeat someone who's made themselves invincible within the system. Hiranyakashyap had all the legitimate authority in the world. The documentation is ammunition, but you need to know when and how to use it—and that might not be through the official channels you're supposed to use.

Build your case not just for internal processes but for external ones—legal action, regulatory bodies, public accountability, whatever leverage exists outside the system the abuser controls.

Build your coalition carefully

Prahlad survived because he had protection beyond what his father could touch. Abusers of power thrive on isolation—making each victim think they're the only one, making each challenger feel unsupported.

Find others who've been harmed. Priya isn't Sharma's only victim. Rahul wasn't either. One person speaking up can be silenced. Many voices, coordinated, are much harder to suppress.

But be strategic. Within a corrupt system, not everyone who seems sympathetic actually is. Some will tell you they support you privately but won't stand with you publicly. Some will use your trust against you.

Find allies outside the system the tyrant controls—colleagues in other departments, contacts at other companies, professional networks, journalists, regulators, lawyers. The wider the circle of accountability, the harder it is for the tyrant to control the narrative.

Challenge from unexpected angles

Narasimha appeared from the pillar—from a direction Hiranyakashyap never anticipated.

Sharma expects complaints to go through channels he controls. He doesn't expect public exposure. He doesn't expect coordinated action from multiple victims. He doesn't expect anyone to go outside the system he's learned to manipulate.

Find the approach he hasn't prepared for. This might mean organizing with others who've been harmed. It might mean finding external accountability mechanisms—regulatory bodies, media, professional organizations, legal channels outside the institution's control. It might mean making the abuse visible to audiences the abuser can't control or intimidate.

The specifics depend on your situation. But the principle remains: if the tyrant controls the system, find ways to operate outside that control.

Channel righteous anger into focused action

Narasimha's fury wasn't aimless. It was directed, purposeful, and ultimately transformative.

Your anger at injustice is valid. Don't suppress it, don't apologize for it, don't let anyone shame you for feeling it. Anger at abuse is the appropriate response.

But channel it. Raw rage without direction burns you out without changing anything. Let yourself feel the full weight of your anger, then ask: where does this energy need to go? What specific action would actually address this injustice?

Priya's anger at watching Rahul be destroyed, at seeing Sharma operate with impunity, at participating through her silence—that anger is information. It's telling her something is wrong and needs to change. The question isn't whether to feel it, but what to do with it.

Protect yourself before you act

Narasimha protected Prahlad before destroying Hiranyakashyap. The child's safety was paramount.

Before you confront power, ensure you have some protection. This isn't cowardice—it's strategy. Martyrdom isn't the goal. Victory is.

Secure what you can first. Build savings if possible. Line up alternative job prospects. Have an exit strategy. Ensure that confronting the abuser won't leave you or your dependents in crisis.

Priya can't confront Sharma if it means her daughter loses education or her mother loses medical care. She needs to prepare first—financial cushion, job alternatives, secured evidence, built coalition.

The pillar exploded at the right moment, not randomly. Timing matters. Preparation matters. Build your position, then act decisively.

Know when formal channels are worth using—and when they're traps

Sometimes official processes work. Sometimes going through proper channels actually delivers justice. But sometimes those channels are designed to exhaust you while protecting the abuser.

Learn to recognize the difference. If the process is genuinely independent, if there's real oversight, if others have successfully used these channels—then they might be worth pursuing.

But if complaints disappear into bureaucracy, if investigators report to the abuser, if whistle-blowers consistently face retaliation despite protections, if the process takes years while the abuse continues—then you're being managed, not heard.

Narasimha didn't petition through proper channels. He broke through when proper channels had failed. Know when you're in a Hiranyakashyap situation—where the system itself is compromised—and adjust accordingly.

Make the cost of tyranny higher than the cost of justice

Hiranyakashyap felt invincible because there was no consequence for his actions. Narasimha changed that calculation permanently.

Abusers of power continue because it works for them. The benefits outweigh the risks. Your job is to change that math.

This might mean making abuse visible to people who care about reputation. It might mean making it expensive through legal action. It might mean making it unsustainable through organized resistance. It might mean making it personally costly through public accountability.

You're not seeking revenge. You're seeking to make tyranny more expensive than justice, abuse more costly than accountability. When that calculation shifts, behavior changes.

Remember you're not trying to destroy a person—you're trying to stop abuse

Narasimha's fury was terrifying, but it was purposeful. He destroyed the tyranny, not randomly or excessively, but precisely what needed destroying.

Your goal isn't to ruin someone's life out of spite. It's to stop the harm they're causing. This is an important distinction because it helps you maintain your own moral compass.

Priya's goal shouldn't be to destroy Sharma as a person. It should be to stop him from harming people, to create accountability, to change the system that enables him. If that results in consequences for him, those are consequences he created through his own actions.

Keep your focus on stopping the abuse, protecting future victims, and creating systemic change. This keeps your anger righteous rather than vengeful, and it helps you know when the fight is done.

What Narasimha Cannot Do

But here's the uncomfortable truth: even if you successfully confront every tyrant, even if you defeat every abuser of power, even if you bring down every corrupt authority figure—you would still face crises that confronting tyranny alone cannot solve.

Because while Narasimha can destroy the demon king, he can't transform the conditions that created him in the first place.

Think about it. Priya successfully brings down Sharma. She documents everything, builds her coalition, finds external accountability, and exposes him. He's fired. Justice is served.

Then what?

Does the company culture that enabled him suddenly change? Do the systems that protected him automatically reform? Does the next manager who takes his place operate differently, or do they simply learn to be more careful about covering their tracks?

Narasimha's fury can break through tyranny. But fury alone doesn't build what comes after.

And here's where the limitations become clear: confronting abuse of power is necessary, but it's not sufficient to create a just world.

You can bring down authoritarian leaders, but if the systems that concentrate power remain unchanged, new authoritarians will rise. You can expose corrupt officials, but if the institutions that enable corruption stay intact, corruption continues. You can defeat individual abusers, but if the culture that protects them persists, abuse persists.

Narasimha teaches you to fight. But he doesn't teach you what to build.

Consider the deeper problems his victory doesn't address:

The massive egos that make people hunger for unchecked power in the first place—Narasimha can destroy those who abuse authority, but he can't humble the ego that seeks to dominate. That requires Vamana's teaching about limits and humility.

The corrupt systems and institutions that make tyranny possible—Narasimha can break through individual instances of abuse, but he can't dismantle the systemic corruption that enables it everywhere. That requires Parashurama's righteous anger directed at dismantling corrupt structures, not just corrupt individuals.

The ethical compromises we're asked to make in confronting evil—Narasimha's fury is so absolute that it's almost frightening. But sometimes the fight against tyranny requires maintaining your own ethical standards even when the tyrant has none. That requires Rama's unwavering commitment to *dharma*, to doing right even when it's costly.

The complex situations where there is no clear tyrant, just impossible choices—Narasimha knows how to destroy clear evil. But what about situations where every option causes harm, where there are no good guys and bad guys, just difficult decisions with real consequences? That requires Krishna's wisdom for navigating moral complexity.

The addiction to outrage and conflict that can develop when you're constantly fighting—Narasimha's fury needs to be calmed eventually. But what happens when fighting becomes your identity, when you can't let go of righteous anger even when the specific battle is won? That requires Buddha's teaching about letting go, about not being consumed by the very struggles that were once necessary.

Priya can defeat Sharma. She should defeat Sharma. The world needs people willing to be Narasimha when Narasimha is called for.

But after Sharma is gone, she'll still work in systems that need transformation. She'll still face leaders with unchecked egos. She'll still encounter institutions more interested in protecting themselves than serving justice. She'll still make difficult ethical choices about how to fight without becoming what she's fighting against.

And she'll need to find a way to live that isn't defined entirely by opposition to tyranny. To build something positive, not just destroy something negative. To create justice, not just punish injustice.

Narasimha gives you the fierce courage to confront abuse of power. Without this, you're complicit in tyranny through your silence. You're enabling what you could stop. You're choosing comfort over justice.

But once you've found that courage? Once you're willing to break through the pillars that need breaking?

Then you need wisdom about what comes next.

The pillar explodes. The demon king falls. The tyranny ends.

But the work of creating a just world? That's only beginning.

And it requires every avatar, working together, each contributing what the others cannot.

* * *

5

Vamana - When Ego Knows No Limits

Anjali sits at the family dinner table, watching her father hold court.

He's telling the story again. The one about how he single-handedly saved the community center from closing fifteen years ago. How the entire neighborhood would have fallen apart without his intervention. How people still thank him for his sacrifice and vision.

Anjali has heard this story a hundred times. She knows the truth: her father donated money, yes, but so did dozens of other families. He served on the committee, but didn't do more work than anyone else. The community center was saved by collective effort, but in her father's telling, he's the hero and everyone else merely helped.

"They wanted to give up," he says, gesturing with his wine glass. "But I told them - I said, 'Not on my watch. This community needs me to lead.' And look at it now. Thriving. All because I refused to accept failure."

Anjali's mother nods approvingly. Her younger brother smiles, completely believing. The dinner guests - neighbors, community members, people who genuinely respect her father - murmur their agreement.

No one contradicts him. No one ever does.

Her father, Rajesh, is a respected figure in their community. Successful businessman. Philanthropist. Served on multiple boards. Known for his "generosity" and "leadership." People seek his advice. They invite him to speak at events. They defer to his opinions on neighborhood matters.

And he believes every word of his own mythology.

"Anjali," he turns to her suddenly. "Tell everyone about your new job."

She tenses. "I'm working at a nonprofit that—"

"A nonprofit," he interrupts, his tone making it clear what he thinks of this choice. "My daughter, who I sent to the best schools, who could have joined my business, decided she wants to 'help people.'" He makes air quotes, smiling indulgently like she's a child going through a phase. "As if that's a real career."

The guests laugh politely, uncomfortably.

"It pays well enough," Anjali says quietly.

"Well enough." He shakes his head. "Do you know how much I make? Do you know how much I could have set you up with? But no, you want to prove something. Always trying to be different from your father."

This is how it always goes. He frames everything as either rebellion against him or tribute to him. Nothing exists outside his orbit.

"I'm proud of the work," Anjali says.

"Proud." He laughs. "You're proud of making 50,000 a year when you could be making three times that? Anjali, pride doesn't pay bills. Pride doesn't buy houses. I didn't raise you to be mediocre."

Her mother touches her father's arm. "Rajesh, let her be. She's young."

"Young and foolish," he mutters, but moves on to another topic - himself. His latest business deal. His opinion on local politics. His views on what the neighborhood needs next.

Everything is about him. Always has been.

Anjali remembers growing up in this house. Every family dinner was her father's stage. Every achievement she or her brother had was really about him - "I pushed you to succeed." Every failure was theirs alone - "I gave you every advantage, how did you mess this up?"

When she was younger, she tried to get his approval. Top grades - "That's expected, not exceptional." Student council president - "I was president of three organizations at your age." Full scholarship to university - "Well, with your last name, they should be honored to have you."

Nothing was ever enough because nothing was ever really about her. It was about reflecting glory back to him.

And the community? They see the polished version. Generous Rajesh who donates to causes. Wise Rajesh who solves disputes. Successful Rajesh who built his business from nothing - except he didn't, he inherited it from his father, but that detail has been quietly edited from his personal narrative.

The guests leave, praising the dinner, thanking Rajesh for his hospitality. On their way out, one woman stops Anjali. "Your father is such an inspiration. You must be so proud."

Anjali smiles. Says yes. What else can she say?

After they leave, her mother starts cleaning up. Anjali helps. Her father sits in his chair, scrolling through his phone - probably checking social media to see if anyone has mentioned him.

"Mom," Anjali says quietly, "don't you ever get tired of it? The stories, the way he makes everything about himself?"

Her mother looks at her sadly. "That's just how he is, dear. He's a great man. Great men have big personalities."

"He's not a great man, Mom. He's a narcissist."

Her mother's face hardens. "Don't speak about your father that way. He's given us everything. This house, your education, respect in the community. You should be grateful."

This is the other part of the trap. The family has been so invested in supporting his ego, in maintaining his image, that questioning him feels like betraying everyone. His ego isn't just his - it's become the family's identity, the community's narrative.

To challenge him is to threaten the whole structure that's been built around him.

Later, Anjali's brother corners her. "Why do you always have to create tension? Dad's proud of what he's built. Is it so hard to just let him have that?"

"He didn't just build it," Anjali says. "And he treats everyone like supporting characters in his personal movie."

"So what? He takes care of us. He's respected. What's the actual problem?"

The actual problem, Anjali realizes, is that her brother can't see it. None of them can. Or they can, but they've decided the benefits of proximity to Rajesh's ego are worth the cost of feeding it.

She thinks about her own life. Chose a career path her father dismisses. Dating someone her father will definitely disapprove of - wrong caste, wrong income level, wrong ambitions. Building a life that isn't about reflecting his glory.

And she's paying for it. The subtle digs at family gatherings. The comparisons to her brother, who joined the family business and validates every choice their father makes. The way her father introduces her to people: "This is my daughter, still figuring things out."

The worst part? She still cares what he thinks. Still wants his approval, even though she knows it'll never come unless she becomes an extension of his ego.

This is what narcissism does. It doesn't just inflate one person. It warps everyone around them. It creates systems where one person's sense of self-importance becomes everyone else's emotional labor. Where questioning the narcissist makes you the problem. Where the family and community protect the ego because they've all invested in it.

Her father isn't cruel, exactly. He provides. He's generous - when it enhances his image. He loves his family - as reflections of himself. He serves the community - in ways that earn him recognition.

But he can't see other people as separate from him. Can't acknowledge limits to what he deserves. Can't share credit or accept responsibility. Can't imagine that the world doesn't revolve around him.

And everyone enables it because he's powerful enough, successful enough, respected enough that challenging him costs more than accommodating him.

Anjali goes home to her small apartment. The one her father called "depressing" when he visited. She looks around at her modest life, built on her own terms, and feels both pride and exhaustion.

She's trying to break free from an orbit. But gravity is strong, especially when the whole family system is designed to keep you spinning around that central sun.

Across the world, millions of people know this dynamic. The narcissistic parent whose ego dominates every family gathering. The community leader whose need for recognition warps every decision. The relative whose sense of entitlement everyone else must accommodate. The person whose ego is so vast that everyone around them becomes smaller to make room for it.

And beneath all of this is a deeper crisis: we've built a culture that celebrates unlimited ego, that confuses narcissism with confidence, that tells people they deserve everything while teaching others to make themselves smaller.

The problem isn't just individual narcissists like Rajesh. It's that we've created systems that produce and reward them.

The Age of Unlimited Ego

We live in an age that celebrates the self to an unprecedented degree.

Social media has given everyone a stage. We curate our lives for public consumption. We count likes, followers, subscribers as measures of worth. We're encouraged to "build our personal brand," to "monetize our influence," to see ourselves as products to be marketed.

"Be your own hero." "You're amazing just as you are." "You deserve everything." "Never settle." "You're the main character in your own story."

These messages are everywhere. And there's truth in them - self-worth, confidence, valuing yourself, these are important. But something has gone wrong in the translation. We've confused healthy self-regard with narcissism. We've mistaken ego for confidence. We've turned "know your worth" into "the world owes you everything."

The result is a culture drowning in ego.

But let's be clear: not everyone with confidence is a narcissist. Not everyone who succeeds is egotistical. Most people are trying their best, balancing self-care with care for others, building lives that matter without demanding the world revolve around them.

But some people - more than ever before, it seems - have lost the plot entirely. They genuinely believe they're exceptional in ways that exempt them from normal human limits. They think their needs supersede others'. They can't imagine a world where they're not the center.

And the systems we've built reward this pathology.

Consider how narcissism operates at different levels.

At the personal level, it's Rajesh. The family member whose ego dominates every interaction. Who can't share credit or accept blame. Who needs constant validation and sees other people's accomplishments as threats to their own importance. Who makes everything about themselves, always, exhaustingly.

Families organize themselves around these egos. Children learn their role is to reflect their parent's glory or serve as cautionary tales of what happens when you don't. Spouses become supporting cast members. Siblings compete for scraps of approval that never quite come.

And here's what makes it so hard to address: the narcissist often provides something. Money, status, connections, stability. Rajesh gives his family a comfortable life and community respect. Challenging him means potentially losing those benefits. So everyone accommodates. Everyone enables. Everyone learns that maintaining his ego is easier than confronting it.

At the community level, it's people like Rajesh in positions of minor power. The HOA president who treats neighborhood governance like a personal territory. The community leader who can't collaborate because they need to be seen as the savior. The volunteer coordinator who does good work but needs everyone to know it's because of their exceptional dedication.

These are the small-scale narcissists who make local life exhausting. Who can't just contribute - they need credit, praise, acknowledgment of their superiority. Who turn community efforts into stages for their ego. Who make working together difficult because everything becomes about managing their feelings and feeding their self-importance.

At the corporate level, it's executives who take credit for their teams' work. Leaders who can't admit mistakes because that would contradict their self-image of infallibility. Bosses who demand loyalty and worship rather than respect and competence. Companies built around founder-worship where one person's vision matters more than thousands of people's labor.

At the wealth level, it's the growing gap between those who have obscene amounts and those who struggle. But it's not just the gap itself - it's the mindset that justifies it. The belief that billionaires "earned" their wealth entirely through merit, ignoring the systems, labor, and luck involved. The conviction that having more money means being more valuable as a human being. The ego that says "I deserve private jets while my workers need food stamps."

At the societal level, it's entire systems built on ego and entitlement. Economic structures that concentrate wealth upward while calling it meritocracy. Political systems where leaders prioritize their image over their constituents' needs. Cultural narratives that tell us success is individual achievement rather than collective effort.

Anjali's entire family has organized itself around Rajesh's ego. Her mother has spent decades supporting his inflated self-image. Her brother has absorbed the same values. Even Anjali, trying to break free, still measures herself against her father's approval. The whole family system runs on the fuel of his narcissism.

Multiply this by millions of families, thousands of workplaces, hundreds of institutions, and you see the scale of the problem.

But here's what's particularly scary about modern ego culture: it's self-justifying.

The narcissist doesn't think they're a narcissist. They think they're exceptional. They genuinely believe their ego is justified by their actual superiority. Rajesh doesn't see himself as self-absorbed - he sees himself as confident, successful, deserving of recognition.

The line between healthy self-esteem and destructive narcissism has blurred. We've lost the wisdom that you can value yourself without devaluing others. That you can be confident without being egotistical. That you can succeed without needing to diminish everyone around you.

We've also lost the wisdom of limits.

In healthier cultures - including the one that created these avatar stories - there was recognition that everyone has a place, a role, boundaries. That no one, no matter how talented or powerful or wealthy, is unlimited. That claiming more than your share, whether of resources or recognition or space, is not success - it's imbalance.

But modern culture says: be limitless. Want more. Achieve more. Deserve more. Never settle. Never be satisfied. Always expand your territory, your influence, your wealth, your importance.

The damage this causes is everywhere.

Anjali sees this clearly now, even if she couldn't name it as a child. Her father's ego isn't just a personality quirk. It's a black hole that swallows everyone else's light. It's a weight everyone in the family carries. It's a story they all perform even though they know it's not true.

And the exhausting part? She still loves him. He's her father. He has good qualities. He provides. He means well, in his limited way.

But his ego makes real love impossible. Real love requires seeing the other person. Rajesh can only see reflections of himself.

We need what the ancient world called Vamana.

The dwarf who reminded a king - gently but absolutely - that everyone has limits. Even kings. Even gods. Even you.

The Dwarf Who Measured the Universe

Long ago, there was a king named Bali. Unlike many kings in these stories, Bali was not evil. He was generous, just, and beloved by his people. He ruled wisely and his kingdom prospered.

But Bali had one flaw: his ego had grown as vast as his kingdom.

Through conquests and righteous rule, Bali had expanded his domain until he controlled all three worlds - earth, heaven, and the space between. He had defeated the gods themselves and claimed their territories. He had performed grand sacrifices that demonstrated his piousness and power. He was, by every measure, extraordinarily successful.

And he knew it.

Bali didn't abuse his power the way tyrants do. He was fair to his subjects, generous with his wealth, dutiful in his religious observances. But he had come to believe something dangerous: that his success proved he deserved unlimited domain. That there should be no constraint on how much he could claim, how far he could expand, how much space he could occupy.

He had begun to confuse his achievements with his worth. To believe that because he could take the three worlds, he should have them. That his power justified his possession of everything.

The gods, displaced from their own realms, appealed to Vishnu. Not because Bali was cruel, but because he had upset the cosmic balance. One being, no matter how accomplished, cannot claim everything without creating imbalance. There must be limits, even for the righteous. Especially for the righteous.

So Vishnu took the form of Vamana - a dwarf, a brahmin boy, small and unassuming.

This is crucial: Vishnu didn't come as a warrior to defeat Bali. Didn't come as a king to match his power. Came as the smallest, most humble form - someone easy to overlook, easy to underestimate, easy to dismiss.

Vamana appeared at one of Bali's great sacrifices, where the king was demonstrating his generosity by granting wishes to holy men. It was a display of his magnanimity, his greatness, his limitless capacity to give.

The small brahmin boy approached the mighty king.

"I have heard of your legendary generosity," Vamana said. "I ask for a small gift. Just three paces of land. Enough space for me to sit and meditate. That's all I need."

Bali's advisors immediately sensed something wrong. "Don't grant this," they warned. "This is no ordinary brahmin. There's power here. Danger."

But Bali's ego wouldn't allow him to refuse. To deny such a small request would make him look petty. And besides, what could a tiny dwarf do with three paces of land? Bali owned three worlds. Three paces were nothing.

"Of course," Bali said magnanimously. "Three paces of land. I grant it."

The moment the promise was made, Vamana began to grow.

He expanded until his form was cosmic, infinite, filling all of space. With his first step, he covered the entire Earth. With his second step, he covered all of heaven and the space between worlds.

He had measured - and claimed - the entire universe in just two steps.

Bali watched in awe and horror. He had promised three paces. Two were taken. One remained.

"Where shall I place my third step?" Vamana asked.

Bali understood. There was nowhere left. Vamana had measured everything Bali claimed to own and shown that it was not Bali's to claim. The king had nothing left to offer except himself.

In that moment, Bali's ego shattered. He saw clearly what he had been blind to: that his success didn't entitle him to unlimited domain. That occupying all space left no room for others. That even his considerable accomplishments didn't mean the universe should revolve around him.

"Place your third step on my head," Bali said, bowing.

And Vamana did. With that final step, he pushed Bali down to the underworld - not as punishment, but as right-sizing. Bali would rule there, fairly and wisely, but within limits. He would no longer claim space that belonged to others. He would no longer confuse his worth with his holdings.

Here's what's remarkable about this story: Vamana didn't destroy Bali. Didn't humiliate him unnecessarily. Didn't take everything from him out of cruelty.

Vamana simply established limits. Said, in effect: "You are accomplished. You are capable. You are worthy of respect. But you are not unlimited. No one is. And claiming to be unlimited doesn't make you great - it makes you unbalanced."

Bali, to his credit, accepted this lesson. He bowed. He recognized his error. He allowed himself to be right-sized without resentment.

The story honors this. Bali is remembered not as a villain, but as a great king who learned humility. He's celebrated annually in festivals. He's respected. But he's respected within limits, not for claiming to be beyond them.

This is the wisdom of Vamana: limits aren't insults. They're necessary. Everyone has them - must have them - for balance to exist. The person who can't accept limits, who genuinely believes they deserve unlimited space, unlimited recognition, unlimited resources - that person is out of harmony with reality itself.

And sometimes, what looks small and humble - a dwarf, a simple request, a gentle question - can reveal the vastness of someone's ego by measuring it against reality.

Vamana didn't need to fight Bali. He just needed to show him the truth: you're not as big as you think you are. The universe doesn't revolve around you. And that's not a diminishment - it's just reality.

Accept it, and you can still be great. Refuse it, and your ego will consume you and everyone around you.

Learning the Lesson of Limits

Anjali doesn't need to hear Vamana's story to understand its truth. She's living it.

Her father is Bali - not the generous, wise king, but the ego that believes it deserves unlimited space. Rajesh has claimed territory in every family interaction, every gathering, every relationship. He's expanded his sense of importance until there's no room left for anyone else to simply be.

And like Bali, Rajesh genuinely doesn't see the problem. He thinks his success justifies his ego. His accomplishments prove he deserves the recognition. His generosity - real as it is - entitles him to dominate every conversation, every decision, every narrative.

He's confused achievement with unlimited worth. Capability with the right to claim everything. Success with exemption from normal human constraints.

The tragedy is that Rajesh could be respected, even honored, if he could accept limits. His actual accomplishments are real. His contributions to the community matter. But his inability to share space, share credit, share the stage makes everything about feeding an ego that's never satisfied.

Anjali has tried being Vamana in small ways. Asking her father to acknowledge others' contributions. Requesting space for her own life choices. Setting boundaries about how he speaks to her.

But unlike Bali, Rajesh doesn't bow. He doesn't recognize the lesson. He sees any limit as an insult, any boundary as rejection, any request for space as evidence of others' ingratitude or inadequacy.

This is where the mythology meets the harder reality of modern life: not everyone learns the lesson. Not everyone accepts being right-sized. Some egos are so defended, so invested in their own narrative of exceptionalism, that they can't see themselves clearly even when confronted with truth.

But that doesn't mean Vamana's wisdom is wrong. It means we need to apply it differently.

What does Vamana teach us about ego, limits, and right-sizing?

He teaches us four essential truths: recognizing actual limits, the power of humility, measuring yourself against reality, and knowing when to step away from unlimited egos.

First, recognizing actual limits

Bali learned that even kings have limits. Even successful, capable, generous people have boundaries to what they can rightfully claim.

For Anjali, this means recognizing that her father's ego isn't actually about his accomplishments. It's about his inability to accept that accomplishments don't entitle you to unlimited recognition, unlimited authority over others' lives, unlimited space in every room.

For all of us, it means understanding that you can be talented, successful, important - and still have limits. Still need to share space. Still have to acknowledge that other people matter too. Still have to accept that the world doesn't revolve around you.

This applies personally: you're not the only person whose needs matter. Your perspective isn't the only valid one. Your pain isn't the only pain that exists. Your success doesn't diminish others' achievements.

It applies professionally: your contributions aren't the only contributions that matter. Your vision doesn't override everyone else's input. Your seniority doesn't mean you're always right.

It applies economically: having more wealth doesn't make you more valuable as a human being. Success doesn't mean you deserve unlimited accumulation while others struggle. Your financial achievements don't exempt you from social responsibility.

Limits aren't insults. They're reality. And accepting them is what allows you to be great in ways that actually matter - in ways that don't require diminishing everyone around you.

Second, the power of humility

Vamana came as a dwarf. The smallest, most humble form. And that small, humble form revealed the vastness of Bali's ego precisely because it was humble.

There's profound power in humility. Not false modesty. Not self-deprecation. But genuine recognition that you're part of something larger, that others matter as much as you do, that your worth doesn't depend on being more important than everyone else.

Anjali chose a nonprofit job that pays less but aligns with her values. Her father sees this as diminishment - "just" 50,000 a year. But Anjali understands something he doesn't: her worth isn't measured by her income or status. She can be valuable without claiming unlimited space.

This is what humility looks like in practice: knowing your worth without needing to prove you're worth more than others. Being confident without being egotistical. Succeeding without needing to dominate. Contributing without needing all the credit.

The most genuinely powerful people - the ones who create lasting positive change - are often the most humble. They don't need to inflate themselves because they're secure in their actual value. They can celebrate others' success because it doesn't threaten their own. They can accept limits because they understand that limits allow balance.

Humility isn't weakness. It's strength that doesn't need constant validation. It's confidence that doesn't require diminishing others. It's success that creates space for more success around it.

Third, measuring yourself against reality

Vamana measured Bali's claim against the actual universe. Two steps covered everything Bali thought he owned. The measurement revealed the truth: Bali's sense of entitlement was vastly larger than what he could rightfully claim.

We all need this measurement against reality. Not against our own inflated self-perception, but against objective truth.

How much credit do you actually deserve for that success? Be honest. Who else contributed? What circumstances helped? What luck was involved?

How much space are you actually taking in relationships? Are you listening as much as you speak? Are others able to shine, or does everything somehow become about you?

How much wealth do you actually need? Not how much you want, not how much you can theoretically accumulate, but how much is actually enough for a good life? What happens to your soul when you claim more than enough while others don't have enough?

This kind of honest self-assessment is difficult. Our egos resist it. We want to believe we earned everything, deserve everything, need everything we have and more.

But Vamana's measurement is always available: look at reality. Look at the actual impact of your ego on others. Look at whether you're sharing space or claiming all of it. Look at whether your sense of deserving matches what you've actually contributed versus what you've extracted from systems and other people's labor.

The measurement will reveal the truth. The question is whether you'll accept it, like Bali, or deny it, like Rajesh.

Fourth, knowing when to step away

Here's the hard truth that Anjali is learning: you can't force someone to accept limits. You can't make a narcissist humble. You can't teach someone who doesn't want to learn.

Bali had the humility to bow. Many people don't.

So sometimes, the wisdom of Vamana means recognizing when you need to step away from someone's unlimited ego. When trying to get them to see reality is futile. When accommodating their ego is costing you your own sense of self.

Anjali is building a life outside her father's orbit. Not to punish him, not out of anger, but because she can't thrive in a space where all the oxygen is consumed by someone else's ego.

This is self-preservation, not selfishness. You're allowed to protect yourself from egos that demand you make yourself smaller. You're allowed to leave relationships where someone else's sense of importance requires you to be unimportant. You're allowed to say "I can't orbit around you anymore."

This doesn't mean cutting off everyone who has an ego. It means recognizing when someone's ego is so defended that they're incapable of seeing you as separate from their reflection. When all the Vamana measurements in the world won't teach them, because they refuse to learn.

Sometimes the wisest thing is to step back, let them have their unlimited self-importance, and build your life in space they don't claim.

What Vamana Would Do Today

How do you cultivate humility, recognize limits, and deal with egos that refuse boundaries?

Here are practices inspired by the dwarf who measured the universe:

Audit your own ego regularly

Before addressing others' egos, examine your own. Ask honestly: Where am I taking more space than I need? Where am I claiming credit that should be shared?

When you tell achievement stories, do you acknowledge the team, circumstances, and luck involved? Or have you edited others out to make yourself the sole hero? In conversations, are you listening as much as speaking? Do you celebrate others' success genuinely, or does it trigger defensive comparisons?

Do this audit monthly. Ego inflation is gradual - a little success here, recognition there, and slowly you believe you're more exceptional than you are. When you find areas where your ego has inflated, adjust immediately. Publicly acknowledge people you've left out. Share credit explicitly. Practice saying "we" instead of "I."

The goal isn't perfection. It's honest self-awareness and course-correction when you drift toward ego inflation.

Take only appropriate space

Vamana asked for three paces - just what he needed. Know what's enough.

In meetings, speak when you have something valuable to contribute, not just to be heard. If you're always the first, longest, or most frequent speaker, that's information. Deliberately hold back. In relationships, your problems don't always get priority just because they're yours. At gatherings, let others tell their stories without redirecting attention to yourself.

With resources, take what you need, not everything you can get. This applies to airtime in conversations, credit for work, money in business, physical space when others need room.

Ask Vamana's question: What's enough? Not what's possible to claim, but what's actually sufficient for your wellbeing without depriving others of meeting theirs?

This is countercultural. We're taught to maximize everything. But taking appropriate space - not all available space - is what allows harmony and balance.

Set clear boundaries with unlimited egos

For people like Rajesh who won't accept limits, boundaries are essential for survival.

Get clear on what you will and won't accommodate. Be specific: "I won't discuss my career with him" or "Family visits are two hours maximum." State these boundaries clearly and calmly as simple facts, not attacks. "I'm not discussing my job anymore." "I'm leaving after two hours."

Don't explain or justify. Explanations become negotiations with narcissists.

Expect pushback. They'll call you ungrateful, selfish, difficult. They'll claim you're the problem. Hold the boundary anyway. Their discomfort with your boundary isn't your responsibility.

When boundaries aren't enough - when someone's ego can't see you as separate from themselves - create distance. Build your own life, relationships, accomplishments that don't require their validation. This isn't punishment; it's survival.

Call out ego gently, then disengage when necessary

Start with gentle measurement: "Can we hear from others now?" "Can you let Sarah finish?" "You've been talking for twenty minutes - I'd like to hear what others think."

These gentle observations often work with people who have some self-awareness. They adjust.

But if someone can't accept gentle measurement, if they react to any limit as an insult, you're dealing with a deeply defended ego. You can try direct confrontation, but often it just creates conflict without change.

Know when to disengage. Recognize when you're dealing with someone whose ego is immovable - who's built their entire identity on being exceptional and beyond normal constraints. Accept them as they are. Maintain your boundaries. Don't sacrifice yourself trying to teach someone determined not to learn.

Resist systems that reward unlimited ego

Individual work matters, but recognize systems that create endless narcissists: economic structures allowing unlimited wealth accumulation, corporate cultures rewarding self-promotion over collaboration, social media designed to amplify ego, educational systems teaching competition over cooperation.

You can't dismantle these alone, but refuse to participate in their values. Support businesses prioritizing community benefit. Vote for leaders showing humility. Build cultures celebrating collaboration. Teach children their worth isn't measured by accumulation or attention.

Every time you share credit genuinely, celebrate others without comparison, acknowledge your limits publicly - you're pushing back against ego culture. Culture changes through accumulated small acts of resistance.

Measure success by limits, not accumulation

Redefine success completely. Not by how much you accumulate, space you claim, or how you compare to others. But by how well you live within appropriate limits. How you contribute while sharing credit. How you succeed while helping others succeed.

Anjali's father measures success by wealth, status, recognition, comparison. He needs to be superior. He can never have enough because there's always another level to achieve.

Anjali measures success differently: alignment with values, positive impact, genuine relationships, internal peace. Her father thinks she's settling. But she has work she believes in, relationships where she's truly known, self-respect that doesn't depend on being superior, the ability to celebrate others' success without feeling diminished.

This is Vamana's offer: freedom from endless ego hunger. Liberation from maintaining an inflated self-image. Permission to be right-sized and discover that's actually enough.

The world worships unlimited ego and calls it greatness. But Vamana stands at three paces and says: this is enough. I can be small and reveal profound truth. I can accept limits and discover that's where real power lives.

You can be small like Vamana and reveal truth. You can bow like Bali and be remembered with honor. You can accept your limits and discover that humility, not ego, is where actual greatness lives.

What Vamana Cannot Do

Even if every narcissist suddenly became humble, even if every ego accepted its limits, even if everyone learned to take only appropriate space—we would still face crises that humility alone cannot solve.

Because while Vamana can teach us to accept limits, he can't dismantle the corrupt systems that concentrate power and wealth regardless of anyone's ego.

Lets imagine. Rajesh becomes genuinely humble. He recognizes his limits, shares credit, makes space for others. He apologizes to Anjali, acknowledges his family's contributions, stops dominating every conversation.

That's beautiful. That heals his family. But does it change the systems that created the massive wealth gap he benefits from? Does it address the institutions that protect the powerful while exploiting the powerless? Does it confront the corruption that allows some to accumulate obscene wealth while others struggle?

Vamana can right-size individuals. But he doesn't dismantle unjust structures.

Consider the deeper problems his lesson doesn't address:

You can have perfectly humble billionaires who accept their limits personally while their companies still exploit workers, destroy the environment, and lobby against regulations. They might be genuinely nice people who don't think they're better than everyone else. But the systems they benefit from and perpetuate? Those systems concentrate wealth and power in ways that harm millions, regardless of how humble the individuals at the top are.

You can have leaders who personally demonstrate humility while presiding over corrupt institutions. They might share credit, acknowledge others, accept limits in their personal conduct. But if the institutions they lead are fundamentally corrupt, their personal humility doesn't fix the structural problems.

You can have people who've learned ego management but still make terrible ethical choices. Humility doesn't automatically grant wisdom about right and wrong. Accepting your limits doesn't tell you what to do in complex moral situations where every option has costs.

Anjali's father becoming humble would transform her family. But it wouldn't address why she earns so little in meaningful nonprofit work while corporate executives extracting value from others' labor earn millions. It wouldn't fix the economic systems that undervalue care work, teaching, social services - the work that actually matters - while richly rewarding ego-driven extraction and exploitation.

And here's another limitation: Vamana teaches acceptance of limits, but he doesn't teach when to fight against limits that are unjustly imposed. Some limits are healthy and necessary - the limits of appropriate space, of what you can rightfully claim, of ego inflation. But other limits are oppressive - the limits society places on people based on gender, race, class, caste. The limits that tell some people they don't deserve as much as others, that their place is smaller, their voice less important, their needs less urgent.

Vamana can't distinguish between accepting appropriate natural limits and resisting unjust imposed limits. He teaches the wisdom of accepting what's enough, but that wisdom can be misused to tell oppressed people they should be satisfied with less than they deserve, that wanting equality is ego, that demanding justice is claiming too much space.

This is the trap: humility is a virtue, but it can be weaponized. "Be humble, accept your place, don't demand more" - this is what the powerful tell the powerless to keep them compliant. And if all we have is Vamana's teaching about accepting limits, we don't have the tools to distinguish between healthy humility and enforced submission.

Anjali needs to learn to take appropriate space and recognize her limits. But she also needs to know when to refuse the limits her father tries to impose - his insistence that her career choice is inadequate, that her worth is measured by his standards, that her life should orbit his approval. Some limits need accepting. Others need fierce rejection.

Vamana doesn't teach which is which.

And he doesn't address what comes after humility. Once you've accepted your limits, once you've learned to take appropriate space, once your ego is right-sized - then what? How do you actually create a just world? How do you dismantle corrupt institutions? How do you navigate complex ethical choices? How do you maintain your integrity when others have none?

Vamana gives you essential foundation. Without humility, without accepting limits, without ego management, you become part of the problem. You become Rajesh, claiming unlimited space and justifying it with your accomplishments. You become the narcissist who damages everyone around you.

But once you have that foundation?

You need Parashurama's sustained commitment to dismantling corrupt systems that concentrate power regardless of individual humility. You need Rama's unwavering ethics to know what's right even when accepting limits might mean accepting injustice. You need Krishna's wisdom to navigate situations where accepting your limits conflicts with demanding justice, where humility conflicts with necessary assertion, where knowing what's enough personally doesn't tell you how to address systemic inequality.

Vamana teaches you to bow. That's crucial. But bowing to reality, to appropriate limits, to the truth that you're not unlimited - that's different from bowing to oppression, to injustice, to systems designed to keep you small.

Learning that difference requires the other avatars.

Humility is necessary. But it's not sufficient. Accepting limits is wisdom. But knowing which limits to accept and which to fight requires wisdom beyond what Vamana offers.

The dwarf measured the universe and taught a king about limits. But the universe still needs people who, having learned their appropriate size, use their right-sized power to create justice, dismantle corruption, uphold ethics, and navigate complexity.

That requires every avatar, working together. Your humility, guided by their wisdom, applied to a world that needs transformation at every level.

Starting with the systems that no amount of personal humility will fix on their own.

* * *

6

Parashurama - When Systems Rot from Within

Keisha sits in the hospital break room, staring at the denial letter.

Mrs. Chen's insurance has rejected coverage for the surgery. Again. Third appeal, third denial. The surgery that could save her life, that her doctors unanimously agree she needs, that's considered standard of care everywhere—denied because the insurance company's algorithm flagged it as "not medically necessary."

Keisha knows what this means. Mrs. Chen, a 62-year-old grandmother who cleaned office buildings for forty years, who finally has insurance through her employer, who thought she was protected—she'll either go bankrupt paying out of pocket or she'll go without the surgery and likely die within a year.

The insurance company will save money either way.

Keisha is a patient advocate. That's her official title. Her actual job is to navigate a system designed to deny care while appearing to provide it. She calls insurance companies, argues with automated systems, appeals denials, translates medical necessity into the specific language these companies require. She's good at her job. She wins more appeals than most.

But she's losing this one. And she knows why.

The insurance company doesn't care about Mrs. Chen. They care about their profit margin, their shareholder returns, their executive bonuses. They've calculated that denying claims—even medically necessary ones—is more profitable than approving them, because most people give up after the first or second denial. The system is designed to exhaust you into submission.

And it's completely legal.

The regulations meant to protect patients have been written by industry lobbyists. The oversight agencies are staffed by former insurance executives. The politicians who could change this receive campaign contributions from the very companies denying care. The system protects itself at every level.

Keisha has worked in healthcare for fifteen years. She became a patient advocate because she believed she could help people navigate a complicated system. She thought if she just learned the rules, mastered the appeals process, understood the regulations, she could make the system work for patients.

But the system isn't complicated. It's corrupt. And it's working exactly as designed—just not for patients.

She thinks about quitting. Every week, she thinks about quitting. But then what? The system doesn't change because she leaves. Someone else takes her job, tries their best, burns out, leaves. The machine keeps running, grinding up vulnerable people, converting their desperation into profit.

Her supervisor, Jennifer, comes into the break room. "Any luck with Mrs. Chen?"

"Denied again."

Jennifer sighs. "I'm sorry. You did everything you could."

"Did I?" Keisha asks. "Or did I just participate in a process designed to look like it offers recourse while actually protecting the company's bottom line?"

Jennifer doesn't answer. What can she say? They both know the truth.

"There's a staff meeting in ten," Jennifer says quietly. "Administration wants to talk about efficiency metrics."

Efficiency metrics. That means they're being pressured to process more cases faster, which means less time per patient, which means lower success rates on appeals. The hospital administration—which claims to advocate for patients—is actually trying to streamline the process of accepting insurance denials because fighting every case costs the hospital money too.

Everyone is optimizing for their own survival within the system. No one is optimizing for patients.

The meeting is exactly what Keisha expected. Charts showing declining appeal success rates. Pressure to "work smarter, not harder." Suggestions to "help patients understand their options"—which means helping them accept that they won't get the care they need and should consider cheaper alternatives or just go without.

One of the newer advocates, Marcus, raises his hand. "What about Mrs. Chen? Her case is clear-cut. The denial is obviously wrong. Can't we escalate to the state insurance commissioner?"

The director of patient services gives him a patient smile. "We could. But that process takes months, sometimes years. And the insurance companies have teams of lawyers. We have to pick our battles."

"So we just let her die?" Marcus asks.

The room goes silent.

"We work within the system we have," the director says carefully. "Not the system we wish we had."

This is the mantra of every institution Keisha has worked in. Work within the system. Be realistic. Don't make waves. Accept that this is how things are.

But how things are is killing people.

After the meeting, Keisha goes back to her desk. She has seventeen other cases waiting. A diabetic man whose insulin coverage was reduced. A child whose therapy sessions were cut from twice weekly to once monthly. An elderly woman whose nursing home care was deemed "custodial" rather than "skilled" and therefore not covered.

Every case is the same story. People who thought insurance meant protection discovering it means profit extraction. A system that appears to provide healthcare but actually provides shareholders with returns. Institutions claiming to serve people while serving themselves.

And everyone inside the system—Keisha, Jennifer, the doctors, the administrators—they're all complicit. Not because they're bad people, but because the system has been built to ensure that doing the right thing is either impossible or so costly that most people can't afford to do it.

She thinks about Mrs. Chen. About her grandchildren who came to the hospital, scared and confused, asking Keisha if their grandma would be okay.

Keisha told them she was doing everything she could. That was true. But "everything she could" within a corrupt system isn't enough.

The system needs to be torn down and rebuilt. But how? Who has the power to do that when the system protects itself at every level? When the people with power benefit from the corruption? When the institutions meant to provide oversight are captured by the industries they're supposed to regulate?

This is the crisis Keisha faces. And it's the crisis millions face in every corrupt institution—healthcare, education, criminal justice, housing, finance. Systems that claim to serve but actually extract. Institutions that appear legitimate but are fundamentally broken. Corruption so deep and systemic that working within the rules means accepting injustice.

The Rot Within Our Institutions

We trust institutions to serve us. That's why they exist, supposedly. Governments to provide justice and public goods. Healthcare systems to heal. Educational institutions to teach. Financial systems to facilitate prosperity. Criminal justice systems to protect and rehabilitate. Housing systems to provide shelter.

But something has gone profoundly wrong.

The institutions that were built to serve people now primarily serve themselves. They've been captured by the interests they were meant to regulate. They've been corrupted not by individual bad actors—though those exist—but by systemic incentives that reward extraction over service, profit over purpose, self-preservation over mission.

This isn't about a few bad apples. It's about the entire orchard being poisoned.

Keisha's experience with healthcare isn't an aberration. It's the system working exactly as designed. Insurance companies maximize profit by denying claims. Hospitals optimize for revenue, not outcomes. Pharmaceutical companies price medications based on what desperate people will pay, not what they cost to produce. The entire system extracts wealth from sick people while claiming to provide care.

And it's protected at every level. Regulations written by industry lobbyists. Oversight agencies staffed by former executives. Politicians funded by corporate donations. Media dependent on pharmaceutical advertising. Every potential check on the system has been captured by the system itself.

This pattern repeats across every major institution.

In education, systems claim to serve students but actually serve bureaucracies, testing companies, and administrative bloat. Schools become compliance machines rather than learning environments. Standardized testing companies profit while teachers struggle. Student loan systems trap young people in debt while enriching lenders. Universities prioritize revenue over education. The corruption isn't hidden—it's just accepted as normal.

In criminal justice, systems claim to serve safety and rehabilitation but actually serve their own growth. Private prisons profit from incarceration. Police departments prioritize revenue through fines and civil asset forfeiture. Prosecutors optimize for conviction rates, not justice. Public defenders are so overwhelmed they can barely represent clients. The system perpetuates itself by creating the conditions that ensure its continued expansion.

In housing, regulatory systems claim to ensure safety and fairness but actually protect established interests. Zoning boards controlled by current property owners block development. Building codes become tools of exclusion rather than safety. Housing agencies serve developers more than residents. The systems meant to provide shelter instead create barriers to it.

In finance, regulatory systems claim to ensure stability and fairness but actually protect the institutions they're supposed to oversee. Regulators come from and return to the industries they regulate. Rules are written to appear tough while containing loopholes. When institutions fail, they're rescued. When individuals suffer, they're told it's their own fault.

The pattern is always the same: institutions that claim to serve actually extract. They've been designed—or have evolved—to benefit those who control them at the expense of those they're meant to serve.

Corruption is systemic, not just individual.

Keisha isn't fighting one bad insurance adjuster. She's fighting an entire system—algorithms designed to deny claims, policies written to maximize rejection rates, legal structures that protect companies from accountability, regulatory capture that prevents oversight, and institutional incentives that reward denying care.

You can't fix this by finding better people to run the system. The system itself shapes behavior. Good people enter corrupt institutions with idealistic intentions and either burn out, become cynical, or slowly adapt to the corruption as "just how things work."

Marcus, the new advocate in Keisha's office, still believes he can make the system work through dedication and clever navigation. Give him a few years. Either he'll quit exhausted and disillusioned, or he'll learn to accept that his job is really just to make an unjust system look fair. To provide the appearance of advocacy while the machine keeps grinding.

Consider how this corruption operates:

Institutions create complexity to hide their corruption. Rules become so intricate that only insiders understand them. Processes require specialized knowledge that keeps outsiders dependent on the system. Appeals and complaints go through channels designed to exhaust rather than resolve. The complexity isn't accidental—it's protective.

Institutions use legitimacy as a shield. They have official processes, professional credentials, legal authority. They publish annual reports showing metrics they've optimized. They claim to follow best practices. The appearance of legitimacy makes it hard to challenge them without seeming unreasonable or uninformed.

Institutions punish those who expose corruption. Whistleblowers lose their jobs and careers. Journalists face lawsuits and intimidation. Advocates are dismissed as troublemakers. The system protects itself by making resistance costly.

Institutions convince people working within them that they're powerless to change anything. "This is just how it works." "We have to be realistic." "Work within the system we have." These mantras train good people to accept corruption as inevitable.

Keisha watches Mrs. Chen—who worked her entire life, who did everything "right," who believed the system would protect her—face a choice between death and bankruptcy because an insurance company's algorithm decided her life isn't worth the expense.

We've learned to navigate information floods, build internal stability, protect the Earth, confront individual tyrants, and manage egos. But what do we do about corruption that isn't individual but systemic? About institutions that aren't temporarily broken but fundamentally captured by the interests they're meant to regulate? About systems designed to protect themselves rather than serve their stated purpose?

We need what the ancient world called Parashurama.

The warrior who didn't reform corrupt systems. Who destroyed them, repeatedly, until the lesson was learned.

Not violence against people. But uncompromising dismantling of corrupt structures. Again and again, until the lesson is learned: institutions must serve their purpose, or they must be rebuilt from the ground up.

The Warrior Who Destroyed Corruption Twenty-One Times

Parashurama's story is unlike the other avatars. It's not a single heroic intervention. It's a pattern repeated, relentlessly, across generations.

His name means "Rama with an axe." And he used that axe twenty-one times to destroy the corrupt warrior class that had forgotten its purpose.

The story begins with injustice, as these stories often do.

Parashurama was born into a brahmin family—priests and teachers, not warriors. His father, Jamadagni, was a sage who lived simply with his wife and sons, devoted to teaching and spiritual practice. They owned a divine cow, Kamadhenu, who provided everything the family needed—not wealth, just sufficiency.

One day, a king named Kartavirya Arjuna visited the ashram. He was a warrior-king, a kshatriya, part of the ruling class whose *dharma*—whose sacred duty—was to protect people, uphold justice, and use power responsibly.

But Kartavirya had forgotten his purpose. He had a thousand arms, symbolizing immense power, and he'd become intoxicated by that power. He saw the divine cow and wanted it. Not because he needed it, but because he could take it.

When Jamadagni refused to give up the cow, Kartavirya simply took it by force. He was the king. He had power. Why should he ask permission?

When Parashurama returned and learned what had happened, he was enraged. Not just at the theft, but at what it represented: a ruler who was supposed to protect the weak had instead used his power to exploit them. A system meant to serve justice had become a tool of oppression.

Parashurama took up his axe—a gift from Shiva—and went to confront the king. He killed Kartavirya Arjuna and retrieved the cow.

But the king's sons sought revenge. While Parashurama was away, they came to the ashram and killed his father, Jamadagni. An innocent sage, murdered by the sons of a corrupt king who couldn't accept consequences for their father's abuse of power.

This is when Parashurama made his vow: he would destroy the corrupt warrior class. Not just these princes, but the entire system they represented. Because the problem wasn't one bad king—it was a class that had collectively forgotten its purpose, that had turned from protectors into oppressors, that used the structures of power meant to serve justice as tools of exploitation.

And he did it. Twenty-one times.

He swept across the land, destroying the warrior class completely. Then they regrew—new rulers, new warriors, new power structures. And they became corrupt again, forgetting their duty, using power for personal gain rather than public service. So Parashurama destroyed them again.

Twenty-one times, the cycle repeated. Power. Corruption. Destruction. Rebuilding. Power. Corruption. Destruction.

Why twenty-one times? Because the lesson kept being forgotten. Because power corrupts, and structures built to serve inevitably get captured by those who benefit from them. Because systems designed to protect people eventually become systems designed to protect themselves and those who control them.

Parashurama represents something uncomfortable: the recognition that some corruption is so deep, so systemic, that reform isn't enough. That sometimes you can't fix the system from within—you have to tear it down and start over.

But here's what's crucial about his story: Parashurama didn't destroy out of personal vendetta. He didn't kill innocents. He didn't attack the warrior class for being warriors—he attacked them for betraying their purpose.

The kshatriyas were supposed to protect. When they became oppressors instead, when they used the system meant to ensure justice to perpetuate injustice, when they forgot they existed to serve rather than to rule—that's when Parashurama acted.

And each time he destroyed the corrupt system, he didn't take power for himself. He didn't declare himself king. He didn't create a new ruling class with himself at the top. He cleared the corruption, then stepped back, allowing new structures to emerge.

The tragedy is that those new structures became corrupt too. Power concentrated. Those meant to serve began to extract. Institutions captured by the interests they were supposed to regulate. The cycle continued.

This is why Parashurama had to act twenty-one times. Not because he failed, but because the problem is ongoing. Corruption isn't a one-time event that can be fixed permanently. It's a constant tendency of systems and institutions—they drift toward serving those who control them rather than their stated purpose.

Parashurama embodies the harsh truth: maintaining just institutions requires constant vigilance and, sometimes, the willingness to tear down what's become corrupted and start again. Not because destruction is good, but because some rot runs so deep that trying to work within the corrupted system only legitimizes and perpetuates it.

His axe isn't a symbol of violence for its own sake. It's a symbol of uncompromising refusal to accept institutional corruption as inevitable or acceptable. It's the willingness to say: this system claims to serve but actually extracts, and it must be dismantled.

The story honors this. Parashurama isn't remembered as a villain or a destroyer. He's remembered as someone who, again and again, refused to let corruption become normal. Who wouldn't accept "this is just how things work" when things worked to harm people. Who understood that sometimes the kindest thing you can do is destroy a system that's causing ongoing harm.

But the story also contains a warning: if you have to destroy corrupt systems twenty-one times, the problem isn't just the systems—it's something deeper about how power works, how institutions drift, how corruption creeps in even when people start with good intentions.

Parashurama cleared the corruption. But he couldn't prevent it from returning. Because he could destroy corrupt structures, but he couldn't change the fundamental dynamics that created corruption in the first place.

That requires more than an axe. That requires the wisdom the other avatars bring.

But first, you need the axe. First, you need the willingness to say: this institution is corrupt, this system has been captured, these structures claiming to serve actually exploit—and they must come down.

When Institutions Betray Their Purpose

Keisha understands Parashurama's fury in a way most people don't. She lives inside a system that claims one purpose while serving another. And she sees, every day, how that betrayal kills people.

The insurance system claims its purpose is to provide healthcare security. That's what people pay for. That's what the industry advertises. That's what regulations are supposed to ensure. But the actual function of the system? To extract maximum profit by denying as much care as possible while maintaining the appearance of coverage.

This is what Parashurama recognized about the warrior class: they claimed to protect but actually exploited. The stated purpose and the actual function had become completely divorced. And the system had built elaborate mechanisms to hide that divorce, to make the exploitation look legitimate, to punish anyone who pointed it out.

The warrior class in Parashurama's time wasn't just individual corrupt kings. It was an entire institutional structure—laws, customs, rules, hierarchies—all designed to concentrate power and protect those who held it. When Kartavirya took the cow, he wasn't breaking the rules. He was using them. The system had been built to allow exactly that kind of extraction.

Just like the insurance system allows—encourages, rewards—the denial of necessary care. The algorithms that reject Mrs. Chen's surgery aren't bugs. They're features. The system is working exactly as designed.

The Pattern Parashurama Saw

This is what made Parashurama different from other warriors who fought individual tyrants. He recognized that the problem wasn't one corrupt king - it was that the entire structure had drifted from its purpose.

Institutions are created with stated purposes: to serve, to protect, to heal, to educate, to ensure justice. Initially, they might even fulfill those purposes. But gradually, inevitably, they drift. Those who control the institution rewrite the rules to serve themselves. Oversight mechanisms get captured. The institution's actual function becomes self-perpetuation and serving those who benefit from it, while the stated purpose becomes just marketing.

Healthcare systems claim to heal—but optimize for profit. Educational systems claim to teach—but serve bureaucratic interests. Criminal justice systems claim to ensure safety—but feed their own growth. Financial regulatory systems claim to ensure stability—but protect the institutions they regulate.

Every institution follows the same trajectory: Purpose. Capture. Corruption. Self-protection.

And here's what makes it so frustrating: the corruption becomes systemic. It's not one bad insurance adjuster denying Mrs. Chen's claim—it's algorithms, policies, regulations, oversight mechanisms, all working together to make that denial not just possible but inevitable. The entire system has been structured to produce that outcome.

Why This Requires More Than Reform

Keisha spent years trying to work within the system. Fighting individual denials. Appealing decisions. Helping patients navigate the bureaucracy. She was good at it - she won cases, saved lives, made a difference.

But slowly, she realized: every victory she achieved was within a system designed to produce defeats. For every Mrs. Chen she helped, ten other patients gave up. The system absorbed her advocacy, learned from it, became slightly better at deflecting it. Her success rate went down even as her skills went up.

This is how captured systems neutralize internal reform. They allow just enough success to make reform seem possible, while the fundamental corruption continues untouched. They co-opt reformers' energy, exhaust them, and use their presence as evidence that "the system works - look, there are advocates, there are appeals, there are channels."

Parashurama understood this. He couldn't fix the warrior class by being a better warrior or by appealing to the warriors' better nature. The whole structure had to come down because the structure itself was the problem.

This is what Keisha is starting to understand. She can't fix healthcare by being a better advocate. The system isn't broken - it's working exactly as it's been designed to work. And that design serves insurance companies, not patients.

What Parashurama's Story Demands

The story of Parashurama makes us deeply uncomfortable because it doesn't offer the comfort of incremental progress. It says: sometimes institutions become so corrupted that reform becomes the only option. Sometimes the most moral action is to stop trying to fix what cannot be fixed and start building alternatives.

This feels extreme. We're taught to work within systems, to be realistic, to pursue incremental change. And sometimes that's right - when institutions are fundamentally sound but temporarily misguided, reform is possible and necessary.

But when institutions have been captured - when their actual function directly contradicts their stated purpose, when every accountability mechanism serves the institution rather than its supposed beneficiaries, when the structure itself perpetuates harm by design - then Parashurama's lesson applies.

He destroyed the corrupt warrior class twenty-one times. Not because he was bloodthirsty, but because corruption kept returning. Even when you clear it, even when you build new structures with good intentions, those structures drift back toward serving those who control them rather than their stated purpose.

The battle to keep institutions serving their stated purpose is never finally won. It requires constant vigilance. And sometimes it requires the courage to say: this has become too corrupt, and it needs to come down so something better can emerge.

This is the wisdom Keisha needs now. Not more skill at navigating a corrupt system, but the clarity to see that the system itself is the problem. Not more resilience to keep fighting losing battles, but the courage to redirect her energy toward building something that actually serves the purpose healthcare claims to serve.

What does that actually look like in practice? How do you recognize when an institution has crossed the line from reformable to requiring dismantlement? How do you build alternatives while the corrupt system still exists? How do you sustain yourself for work that Parashurama had to repeat twenty-one times?

That's the practical wisdom he offers.

What Parashurama Would Do Today

To be a Parashurama is tricky. How do you recognize institutional corruption, refuse to enable it, and work toward building something better?

Here are practices inspired by the warrior who destroyed corrupt systems twenty-one times:

Learn to recognize institutional betrayal of purpose

Before you can address corruption, you need to see it clearly. Parashurama recognized when the warrior class had drifted from protection to exploitation. You need this same clarity about institutions.

Ask: What is this institution's stated purpose? What does it claim to do? Then ask: What does it actually do? Who does it actually serve?

For healthcare: Claims to provide care and security. Actually maximizes profit through denial and extraction.

For your local institution—school, government agency, company, whatever—do the same analysis. If there's a significant gap between stated purpose and actual function, that's your first signal.

Then ask: Who benefits from this institution as it currently operates? If the answer is "primarily those who control it" rather than "those it claims to serve," you've identified institutional corruption.

Document this. Write it down. Be specific. Not "the system is bad" but "this institution claims X purpose but actually does Y, which serves Z interests." Clarity protects you from being gaslit by the institution's own propaganda about itself.

Identify the capture mechanisms

Keisha's healthcare system stays corrupt because every accountability mechanism has been captured. Parashurama saw that the warrior class protected itself through laws, customs, and structures that prevented challenge.

Look for how your institution protects itself:

- Who writes the rules? (Often the regulated write regulations)
- Who provides oversight? (Often former/future industry insiders)
- Who funds the politicians who could change things? (Often the institution itself)
- Where do regulators go after their "public service"? (Often to the industry they regulated)
- What happens to whistleblowers? (Often they're punished while the institution is protected)

Map the connections. See how the institution has neutralized every mechanism that could hold it accountable. Understanding the capture helps you see why reform from within won't work—the institution has made sure internal reform is impossible.

Stop legitimizing corrupt systems

This is hard, but essential: recognize when your participation in a corrupt system legitimizes it.

Keisha helps patients navigate insurance denials. This is compassionate—people need help. But it also makes the system look fair: "Look, there's an appeals process, there are advocates, there are channels." Her good work provides cover for a fundamentally corrupt system.

Sometimes the most moral thing is to stop participating. Stop making the corrupt system look functional. Stop providing the fig leaf of legitimacy.

This doesn't mean abandon the people harmed by the system. It means be honest about what you're doing: you're helping individuals survive a corrupt system, not making the system work. And consider whether your efforts could be better spent building alternatives rather than propping up corruption.

If you work inside a corrupt institution, consider: Am I actually changing anything, or am I just providing the appearance of accountability while the institution continues harming people? If it's the latter, leaving might be more ethical than staying—even though leaving is hard, costly, and won't directly help those the institution harms.

Build and support alternatives

Parashurama didn't just destroy—he made space for new structures. You can't just tear down corrupt systems; you need to build alternatives that actually serve their stated purpose.

This looks different in different contexts:

For healthcare: Support mutual aid networks, direct primary care, community health clinics, single-payer advocacy—systems that don't have profit-extraction at their core.

For education: Support alternative schools, homeschool cooperatives, community learning spaces—structures designed to educate rather than credential and process.

For housing: Support housing cooperatives, community land trusts, mutual aid—models where inhabitants control housing rather than investors extracting wealth.

For any corrupt institution: Look for or help create alternatives that actually serve the stated purpose the institution has abandoned. Put your time, money, and energy there rather than trying to reform the unreformable.

These alternatives often start small and scrappy. That's fine. They're building what's needed rather than maintaining what's corrupt. Even if they fail, they demonstrate that another way is possible.

Expose corruption publicly and clearly

Parashurama didn't hide what he was doing or why. He made it clear: this class has betrayed its purpose and must end.

If you see institutional corruption clearly, say so publicly. Not vaguely—"the system has problems"—but specifically: "This institution claims to do X but actually does Y, which serves Z interests at the expense of the people it claims to serve."

Use whatever platform you have. Write articles. Speak at meetings. Post online. Talk to journalists. File complaints—not because you think captured oversight will help, but to create a public record. Testify when there are hearings. Make the corruption visible.

Expect pushback. Corrupt institutions attack those who expose them. They'll call you uninformed, unrealistic, troublemaker. They'll question your motives. They'll threaten consequences.

Protect yourself as much as possible—document everything, build support networks, know your legal rights. But don't let fear of institutional retaliation silence you. That fear is how corruption maintains itself.

Support whistleblowers and reformers

People inside corrupt institutions who try to expose or change them face enormous pressure. They risk their careers, their reputations, their livelihoods.

When someone blows the whistle on institutional corruption, support them. Publicly, if possible. Financially, if they face retaliation. By amplifying their message, sharing their story, making sure they're not isolated.

When someone inside an institution tries to reform it—even if you think the institution is beyond reform—support them too. They're doing important work even if it ultimately fails. They're demonstrating that people with integrity exist inside corrupt systems. They're making the corruption visible by contrast.

Don't let institutions isolate their challengers. That's how they neutralize threat—by making challengers fight alone, get exhausted, and give up or get pushed out.

Know when dismantling is necessary

This is the hardest wisdom. Sometimes institutions are so corrupted, so captured, so structured around self-service that they cannot be reformed. Trying to reform them wastes energy that could build alternatives.

How do you know when an institution has crossed this line? Ask:

- Has every accountability mechanism been captured by the institution?
- Do efforts to reform get co-opted or exhausted by the system?
- Does the institution spend more energy protecting itself than serving its purpose?
- Would people be better served by building alternatives than fixing this?

If the answers are yes, then Parashurama's lesson applies: stop trying to fix it. Work to dismantle it while building better alternatives.

This doesn't mean violence against people or property. It means withdrawing legitimacy, building alternatives, supporting political movements to defund or eliminate the corrupt institution, and refusing to perpetuate the lie that it can be reformed.

Sometimes the most compassionate thing is to stop propping up structures that harm people. Sometimes the most constructive thing is to clear away what's corrupt so something better can emerge.

Accept that this is ongoing work

Parashurama destroyed corrupt systems twenty-one times. The work didn't end. New corruption emerged. New systems betrayed their purpose. The fight continued.

This is demoralizing if you think you're trying to solve corruption permanently. It's sustainable if you understand you're maintaining pressure against corruption's constant tendency to emerge.

You're not going to fix all institutional corruption in your lifetime. But you can refuse to enable it. You can build alternatives. You can expose it. You can support others doing the same. You can be one person in a long line of people saying "no, this has betrayed its purpose" and working to tear down what needs tearing down.

The institutions you help dismantle might eventually become corrupt again. That doesn't make your work meaningless. It makes it part of an ongoing cycle of accountability—people keep institutions honest by being willing to tear them down when they become corrupt.

Be Parashurama. See corruption clearly. Refuse to enable it. Build alternatives. Expose betrayal. Support challengers. And when institutions have become too corrupt to reform, have the courage to say so and work toward something better.

The axe isn't violence. It's clarity. It's refusal. It's the uncompromising commitment to purpose over structure, to service over self-perpetuation, to building what works over preserving what's corrupt.

What Parashurama Cannot Do

Keisha successfully helps dismantle the corrupt healthcare insurance system. People organize, build alternatives, create political will, and the profit-driven model is replaced with something designed to actually provide care rather than extract wealth.

The corrupt institution is gone. Now what?

How do you build the replacement? What principles guide resource allocation when care is scarce? Who decides what's ethical when treatments are experimental? When values conflict—autonomy versus paternalism, individual choice versus collective good—how do you navigate that?

This is where Parashurama's wisdom ends. He destroyed the corrupt warrior class twenty-one times but never provided guidance for building systems that would resist corruption. He had the axe to tear down what betrayed its purpose. But constructing something better? That's different wisdom.

The pattern of his story reveals the problem: destroy, rebuild, watch it corrupt, destroy again. Twenty-one cycles. If simply tearing down and starting over worked, once would have been enough. The fact that corruption kept returning suggests destruction alone isn't the solution.

Something deeper needs to change—not just which institutions exist, but how institutions resist the drift from purpose to self-service. Not just who holds power, but how power itself operates without corrupting those who wield it.

Parashurama can't teach this because his tool is destruction, not construction or maintenance. The axe clears corruption but doesn't prevent its return.

Consider what his approach leaves unaddressed:

The new healthcare system Keisha helps build will be designed by people. If those people have unchecked egos, believing they're exceptions to normal constraints, entitled to unlimited authority—the new institution will corrupt just like the old one. Dismantling doesn't solve ego. Vamana's teaching about limits does.

The new system will face difficult choices where the ethical path isn't obvious. Experimental treatments that might help or harm. Resource allocation during shortages. Competing rights and responsibilities. When doing the right thing costs you power, position, or resources—when integrity is painful—will the new institution compromise like the old one did? Parashurama deals in clarity: this is corrupt, end it. But navigating moral ambiguity when there's no obviously right answer? That's Krishna's wisdom, not his.

Even people committed to building just institutions can lose their way if they're addicted to the comfort, status, or identity that came from the old corrupt systems. Parashurama destroys external structures, but what about the internal attachments that keep you participating in corruption even when you know better? Buddha addresses that; Parashurama doesn't.

And maintaining ethical integrity across time, especially when it's costly? When standing on principle means losing ground to those who compromise? The new institutions need people who won't sacrifice purpose for survival. Rama embodies that unwavering commitment to what's right even when it hurts. Parashurama only teaches when to destroy, not how to maintain.

Most fundamentally: if you have to tear down corrupted systems repeatedly, clearly something about the cycle itself needs transformation. Not just fighting this instance of corruption or that one, but understanding what makes institutions drift from their purpose and preventing it. Kalki represents that deeper transformation—changing not just the specific corrupt structures but the patterns that create corruption.

Keisha needs Parashurama's courage to stop enabling corrupt systems and work toward dismantling them. Without that willingness to say "this cannot be reformed and must end," she's trapped maintaining corruption forever.

But once the corrupt system is gone, she needs wisdom Parashurama doesn't provide: How to build replacements that resist capture. How to maintain purpose when institutions naturally drift toward self-service. How to structure power so it serves rather than exploits. How to navigate complex ethics without clear answers. How to free people from attachments to what needs dismantling.

The warrior clears space. The other avatars teach us what to build in that space and how to keep it from becoming what we just destroyed.

* * *

7

Rama - When Integrity
Has a Price

Michael sits in his car outside the newsroom, staring at the USB drive in his hand.

On this drive is a story that will change everything. Six months of investigation. Dozens of interviews. Documents, emails, financial records. Proof that the city's largest employer—a tech company that provides 40% of local jobs and funds half the city's budget through taxes—has been systematically evading environmental regulations, dumping toxic waste into the water supply, and bribing inspectors to look the other way.

It's the story of his career. The story every investigative journalist dreams of. Airtight evidence. Undeniable truth. The kind of reporting that wins awards, that matters, that actually changes things.

He's been working on it since he found the first leaked document. Nights, weekends, vacation days. Following leads, confirming sources, building the case piece by piece. His editor, Peter, knew he was working on something but didn't ask for details—he trusted his process.

Yesterday, he finally told him. Laid out everything. Showed him the evidence. Watched his face change as he realized the implications.

"This is incredible work, Michael. Really. But we can't run it."

He'd expected pushback. Expected to have to defend the sourcing, the evidence, the story's readiness. He didn't expect this.

"The company will pull all their advertising. That's $4 million a year—a third of our revenue. They'll sue us. They have unlimited legal resources; we have a budget. And..." Peter paused. "The publisher's son-in-law works there. In a senior position. This story will destroy his career."

"But it's true. Everything is documented. This isn't opinion, it's fact. People are being poisoned. Children are drinking contaminated water."

"I know. And if we were a different paper, with different financial realities, maybe we could run it. But we're barely surviving as it is. If we lose that ad revenue, we fold. Everyone here loses their jobs. No newspaper means no watchdog for any story in this city."

"So we protect them because they pay us?"

Peter looked tired. "We protect our ability to keep existing. Sometimes you have to compromise on one story to be able to report on others. That's the reality of this business."

Michael left his office. Went to the publisher. Got the same answer, more bluntly: "We're not running a story that destroys our biggest advertiser and embarrasses my family. Find something else to work on."

He's been sitting in this parking lot for twenty minutes. He has options. He could leak it to a national paper—they'd love the story, have the resources to defend against lawsuits, don't depend on local advertising. He could post it online himself—the evidence is solid enough to speak for itself.

But there are consequences.

His contract has a non-compete clause. If he leaks the story, the paper will sue him for breach. He'll lose his job, his severance, probably his savings in legal fees. He'll be blacklisted—no local outlet will hire someone who burned their employer. He'd have to move, start over somewhere else, if anyone will hire him at all.

And it's not just him. His wife, Jennifer, just got promoted to principal at the high school. It's the job she's worked toward for fifteen years. If he blows up the city's largest employer, if he forces the paper to close, if he becomes the person who cost hundreds of people their jobs—Jennifer will be collateral damage. The school board won't keep a principal whose husband destroyed the local economy.

His parents live here. His friends. His whole life. Everything he's built over fifteen years in this city.

He thinks about his daughter asking him what he does for work. "I'm a journalist, sweetie. I tell people the truth about what's happening in the world." She drew a picture of him as a superhero once, with a newspaper wrapped like a cape.

Can he look at her and say he's a journalist who knew the truth and stayed silent because telling it was too expensive?

But he also thinks about her asking why they had to move, why Mom had to quit her job, why Dad doesn't work anymore, why everything changed. He thinks about Jennifer losing the job she's worked for her whole career. About starting over at 38 in a new city where no one knows him. About his parents asking why he threw away everything over one story. About the newsroom colleagues who'll lose their jobs when the paper folds.

This is the choice: Tell the truth and lose everything. Or stay silent and keep his life.

Everyone keeps telling him the answer is obvious. His editor says keep your job, you can still do good work. His publisher says it's not your responsibility to destroy yourself. His wife says whatever you decide, but reminds him they have a life here. His practical mind says one story isn't worth your entire career.

But somewhere inside, in the part of him that became a journalist because he believed in truth, a voice keeps asking: If not you, who? If not now, when? If you stay silent when you know the truth, what are you?

He's been sitting here long enough that people are starting to notice. He needs to decide. Keep the USB drive, leak the story, burn everything down. Or go inside, delete the files, tell Peter he understands, and accept that this is how the world works.

Integrity or survival. Truth or everything he's built.

Michael takes a breath, picks up his bag, and opens the car door.

The question hanging in the air: What kind of journalist is he? What kind of person?

The Crisis of Integrity

Like our previous stories, Michael's dilemma isn't unique. It's the story playing out in millions of lives, across every profession, every industry, every institution.

The accountant who discovers their firm is helping clients hide money offshore. Report it and lose your partnership track, your bonus, your career trajectory. Stay silent and you're complicit, but you keep your mortgage payment.

The engineer who finds a safety flaw in a product about to ship. Flag it and the launch delays, the company loses market position, shareholders get angry, and you become "not a team player." Sign off anyway and nothing probably happens - probably - and you keep your reputation as someone who delivers.

The teacher who's told to pass students who haven't earned it because the school's funding depends on graduation rates. Fail them honestly and you're hurting the entire school, every other student, your colleagues who depend on those resources. Give them the grades and you're just being realistic about how education works now.

The lawyer who realizes their client is lying but already took the retainer. Withdraw from the case and you breach ethics rules, damage your reputation, and lose the biggest fee of your career. Continue representing them and you're just doing your job - everyone deserves legal representation, right?

We've built a world where doing the right thing consistently costs too much for most people to afford.

The language has changed to make this easier. We don't call it lying anymore - it's "strategic communication" or "managing the narrative." We don't call it corruption - it's "networking" or "relationship building" or "understanding the realities of business." We don't call it cowardice - it's "picking your battles" or "being pragmatic" or "thinking long-term."

We've become experts at explaining why doing wrong is actually smart, why compromise is actually wisdom, why integrity is actually a luxury that responsible people can't afford.

And we have good reasons. Real reasons. The stakes are genuine.

Michael isn't choosing between truth and lies in some abstract philosophical sense. He's choosing between exposing environmental poisoning and keeping his wife's career intact. Between protecting children's health and protecting his own child's stability. Between being a good journalist and being a good husband, father, son.

These aren't easy choices. They're not choices between obvious good and obvious evil. They're choices where every option has real costs and real consequences for real people you love.

This is what makes modern ethical erosion so subtle. It doesn't announce itself. It doesn't show up as a dramatic moment where a villain asks you to betray everything you believe. It shows up as your boss saying "let's be realistic," as your spouse saying "we have responsibilities," as your own mind saying "one compromise won't make you a bad person."

And it's not one big compromise. It's a thousand small ones. Each individually justifiable. Each slightly easier than the last. Each creating a precedent that makes the next one feel inevitable.

You compromise once because the alternative is too expensive. Then you compromise again because you've already compromised before - might as well be consistent. Then you compromise again because that's just who you are now, someone who compromises, so fighting it would be hypocritical. Then one day you look in the mirror and realize you've become someone who doesn't even see most compromises anymore. They're just how you operate. How everyone operates.

If every accountant reported every irregularity, if every engineer flagged every flaw, if every journalist exposed every wrongdoing, if every employee spoke up about every unethical practice - the whole apparatus would grind to a halt. We've built an economy, a society, a way of life that requires a certain amount of convenient blindness to function.

We know this. And it paralyzes us.

We tell ourselves that one person can't change the system, that our individual choice doesn't matter, that someone else will step up. But everyone is telling themselves the same thing, and no one steps up, and the system persists.

This is the crisis Michael represents. Not one journalist's dilemma, but humanity's dilemma. What do we do when we know what's right but doing it will cost us everything? When our ethics have a price tag we can't afford? When being a good person conflicts with being a surviving person?

In the ancient World, there was a prince who faced exactly this choice. Who had to decide between his kingdom and his integrity. Between power and principle. Between everything he'd been given and everything he believed in.

His name was Rama. And his choice echoes across millennia as one of the most important stories humanity has ever told about what it means to be human.

The Prince Who Chose Principle Over Everything

Thousands of years ago, in the kingdom of Ayodhya, there lived a prince named Rama.

He was everything a kingdom could hope for in its future king. Skilled in warfare, wise in counsel, beloved by the people. His father, King Dasharath, had announced that Rama would be crowned king the next day. The entire kingdom was celebrating.

That night, everything changed.

Dasharath's youngest wife, Kaikeyi, reminded the king of two promises he'd made to her years ago - that he would grant her any two wishes she asked for. She'd saved those promises, waiting for the right moment. Now she was ready to use them.

Her first wish: Crown my son Bharat as king instead of Rama. Her second wish: Send Rama into exile in the forest for fourteen years.

Dasharath was devastated. Rama was the rightful heir, the capable heir, the one the kingdom needed and wanted. Bharat himself didn't want the throne - he loved his brother and thought this was wrong. The entire court was in uproar. The people were ready to revolt. Rama's mother, Kaushalya was in anguish.

And Rama? He had a choice to make.

He could have said no. He had the army's loyalty, the people's support, the court's backing. His father's promise was made under manipulation - Kaikeyi had waited until the eve of coronation to spring this trap. Any legal scholar would have found grounds to invalidate it. Any political advisor would have said this was tyranny masquerading as tradition.

Rama could have taken the throne. Everyone wanted him to. Everyone expected him to. It was the practical choice, the smart choice, the choice that would have saved the kingdom from chaos.

But there was one problem: his father had given his word.

The promise might have been manipulated. It might have been unfair. It might have been destructive. But it had been given. And if Rama became king by breaking his father's word - what kind of king would he be? What kind of example would he set? What would his rule be built on?

If *dharma* - righteous conduct, ethical duty, doing what's right - could be bent when it was inconvenient, when was it real? If promises could be broken when keeping them was costly, what did promises mean?

So Rama made his choice.

He gave up the throne. He gave up the palace, the comfort, the power, everything he'd been raised to inherit. He put on the simple clothes of a forest ascetic, took his bow, and walked away from the kingdom that should have been his.

His wife Sita and his brother Lakshman insisted on joining him. For fourteen years, they lived in exile. The crown prince became a forest dweller. The future king became a wanderer.

And through those years, Rama maintained his integrity. When other kings offered him armies to take back his throne, he refused. When circumstances changed that could have justified returning early, he stayed. When the fourteen years ended exactly, not a day early despite all he'd suffered, he returned.

He kept his father's word even though it cost him everything.

But the story doesn't end there. Because integrity sometimes demands even more than we think we can give.

The Second Test

During exile, Sita was kidnapped by Ravan, the demon king of Lanka. Rama waged war, defeated Ravan, rescued Sita. It was a victory that should have ended with celebration.

Instead, Rama faced another impossible choice.

The people of Ayodhya whispered. Sita had been held captive in another man's palace for months. How could they be sure of her purity? How could the kingdom accept a queen whose virtue had been questioned? The murmurs grew louder, the doubts more public.

Rama knew Sita was pure. He trusted her completely. He had fought a war to get her back. But he was also a king now, returned from exile, responsible not just to his heart but to his kingdom. And the kingdom had doubts.

So he asked Sita to undergo Agnipariksha - the trial by fire. To prove her purity by walking through flames.

Imagine that moment. Imagine being Sita, who had waited faithfully, who had refused Ravan's advances, who had maintained her integrity in captivity - now being asked by her own husband to prove herself.

Imagine being Rama, who knew the truth but felt bound by duty to his role as king, to public expectation, to what leadership demanded.

Sita agreed. She walked into the fire. And the fire itself testified to her purity - she emerged unharmed, vindicated.

But the cost of that choice echoed through their lives. Some versions of the story say Sita never fully forgave being doubted. Some say Rama never fully forgave himself for doubting. Some say the marriage was never quite the same after integrity demanded such a painful price.

This is what makes Rama's story so important, and so difficult.

He wasn't wrong to keep his father's word - that exile taught him what it means to be a true leader, stripped him of privilege and showed him his people's lives. He wasn't wrong to be concerned about his kingdom's doubts - a king does have responsibilities beyond personal preference.

But integrity came at a cost that perhaps shouldn't have been paid. Doing the right thing created consequences that rippled through lives and caused real pain to real people who deserved better.

The Question Rama's Story Asks

This is the story we remember thousands of years later. Not because Rama was perfect. Not because every choice he made was unambiguously correct. But because he faced the question that defines what it means to be human:

When doing the right thing costs you everything - your comfort, your power, your relationships, your happiness - do you still do it?

When your principles conflict with your survival, which do you choose?

When integrity has a price tag you can barely afford to pay, do you pay it anyway?

Rama's answer was yes. Even when it meant exile. Even when it meant personal anguish. Even when it meant making choices that haunted him.

He chose *dharma* - righteous conduct, ethical duty, doing what's right - over everything else.

Not because it was easy. Not because it didn't cost him. Not because he didn't suffer for it.

But because he believed that who you are is determined by what you do when doing the right thing costs you everything.

When Integrity Demands Everything

Michael opens his car door. He's going to leak the story.

Not because he's naive about the cost. He knows exactly what he's losing. His job, probably his marriage, definitely his life as he knows it. He's going to do it anyway.

Because he just realized something sitting in that parking lot: he's already made this choice. Years ago, when he became a journalist. When he told his daughter what he does for a living. When he built his whole identity around telling the truth.

The person who stays silent to protect his career isn't a journalist who made a smart tactical choice. It's someone who stopped being a journalist the moment the work got expensive.

This is what Rama understood. He didn't agonize over whether giving up the throne was worth it. The question was: can I be who I say I am and do this other thing? The answer was no. So the choice was already made.

The Choice Rama Made

When Rama stood in that palace facing exile, everyone gave him the same advice Michael's been getting. Be smart. Be strategic. Take the throne now, fix things from a position of power, honor your father's word in other ways later.

It all sounded reasonable. It was all the same trap.

Because Rama saw what Michael just saw: if you compromise your integrity to preserve your position, you no longer have integrity to bring to that position. If you become king by breaking your father's word, you become a king whose word can be broken. If you take power by explaining why principles don't apply this time, you become a ruler whose principles don't apply when it's inconvenient.

The fourteen years in exile weren't punishment for choosing right. They were the cost of being who he was. And they taught him what he needed to know - what it meant to live without privilege, to rely on himself, to see his kingdom from the perspective of those who had nothing. He returned a better king because he'd paid the price of his principles.

But the story doesn't end there.

The Agnipariksha - asking Sita to prove herself through fire - shows us something harder. Because that choice was also made from integrity, from duty, from doing what Rama thought was right. And it caused terrible pain. It satisfied one form of righteousness while violating another.

Was he right? The story doesn't tell us. Some say Sita never forgave being doubted. Some say the marriage was never the same. Doing the right thing doesn't mean everything works out perfectly. It means you become who you need to be, and you live with the consequences.

What This Means for Michael

Michael walks back into the newsroom. He doesn't go to his desk. He goes straight to Peter's office.

"I'm leaking the story," he says. "Not to punish you or the paper. But because I can't be a journalist who knows the truth and stays silent. That's not a journalist anymore. That's someone else."

Peter nods slowly. "You know what this will cost you."

"Yeah. But I know what the other choice costs too. And I can't afford that price."

Here's what Michael understands now, what took Rama fourteen years in a forest to learn: you can't control outcomes, but you can control your character. You can't know if your integrity will change the world. You can only know whether it changes you.

If Michael stays silent, he becomes someone who chose comfort over truth. That person will face easier choices in the future - because he's already established that truth has a price limit. Every subsequent compromise will be simpler, more automatic, until one day he won't even recognize the question anymore.

If he speaks, he becomes someone who stood for something when it cost everything. That person might pay dearly. But he gets to be that person. And maybe his daughter will understand, years from now, why Dad threw everything away over one story. Because some things matter more than keeping what you have.

The Price Is Real

Jennifer will be furious. His parents will think he's lost his mind. His colleagues will think he's destroyed their livelihoods over self-righteous principle. They might all be right.

Rama's story doesn't promise that choosing integrity makes everything work out. It promises that choosing integrity makes you the person who chose integrity. That's all. That's everything.

The exile was real. The pain was real. The cost was real. And when Rama returned to be crowned king - finally, after fourteen years - he was someone different than the prince who could have taken the throne that first night. He'd paid for his principles in ways that changed him. Made him worthy of the crown in ways he hadn't been before.

Michael doesn't know what comes next. Maybe the story changes things. Maybe it gets buried. Maybe he's destroying his life for nothing. But he knows one thing: he needs to be able to look at himself in the mirror. And he needs his daughter to know that when he told her he tells people the truth, he meant it.

Even when telling the truth costs him everything he has.

That's the choice Rama made. Not once, but again and again. First with the exile. Then with the Agnipariksha. Each time doing what he believed was right even when it destroyed him. Each time accepting that integrity isn't what you do when it's convenient - it's precisely what you do when it's not.

What Rama Teaches

Rama doesn't teach that integrity is easy or cost-free. He teaches that integrity is who you are when the price is too high to pay.

He doesn't teach that doing right means everything works out. He teaches that becoming someone who abandons their principles when tested costs more than any job, any comfort, any security ever could.

He doesn't teach that you'll never regret your choices. He teaches that you can live with regret about what you lost more easily than you can live with becoming someone you don't recognize.

Michael is about to find out if that's true. He's about to pay the price of being a journalist when journalism is expensive. The price of telling the truth when truth destroys your life. The price of integrity in a world built to punish it.

Rama paid that price. He survived it. He became who he needed to be because of it.

Maybe Michael will too.

What Rama Would Do Today

So you're facing your own version of Michael's parking lot. Your own moment where doing what's right will cost you more than you think you can afford. What does Rama's example actually teach you?

Not generic advice about integrity. Something more specific. Something harder.

Recognize that you've already made the choice

Michael thought he was deciding whether to leak the story. He wasn't. He'd already decided when he became a journalist, when he spent six months investigating, when he told his daughter what he does for work.

The question wasn't "should I do this?" The question was "can I be who I say I am and not do this?" And the answer was no.

This is Rama's first teaching: you don't decide your principles in the moment of crisis. You discover what principles you've already committed to.

When you're facing your impossible choice - whether to report the misconduct, whether to refuse the unethical assignment, whether to speak up when staying silent would be safer - stop asking "what should I do?" Ask instead: "Who am I?"

If you're someone who tells the truth, there's no decision to make. If you're someone who maintains integrity, the choice is already clear. The only question is whether you have the courage to be who you already are.

If you're not sure who you are - if your principles are vague generalities you've never tested - then you'll make the choice under pressure, tired, scared, with everything on the line. And you'll probably compromise.

Define who you are before the test comes. Then when it arrives, you're not deciding - you're remembering.

Accept that you can't have it both ways

Everyone will tell you there's a middle path. A way to maintain your integrity and keep your job. A compromise that honors your principles without costing you everything.

They're lying. Or they're lying to themselves.

Rama could have said "I'll take the throne now to prevent chaos, but I'll honor my father in other ways." It sounds reasonable. It's the trap that destroys integrity.

Because if you compromise your integrity to preserve your position, you no longer have integrity to bring to that position. The person who takes the throne by breaking promises becomes a king whose promises can be broken. The journalist who stays silent to keep his platform becomes a journalist whose truth has a price tag.

You cannot do the wrong thing for the right reasons and remain who you claim to be.

When you're tempted by the "middle path" - when someone says you can honor your principles and protect your interests if you're just clever enough about it - recognize it for what it is. A way to feel good about compromise. A way to betray yourself while claiming wisdom.

Rama's teaching is uncompromising: you're either someone who keeps their word even when it destroys you, or you're not. There's no third option that lets you be both.

Count the real cost, not just what you're losing

Michael is counting what leaking the story will cost: his job, his wife's career, his reputation, his stability, his life as he knows it.

But he needs to count what staying silent will cost too: becoming someone who chose comfort over truth. Living with the knowledge that he knew and said nothing. Watching children drink poisoned water while he protected his career. Looking at his daughter knowing he lied about who he is.

Those costs are real. They're just harder to see because they don't show up on a spreadsheet.

Rama spent fourteen years in exile. That's a real cost anyone can see. But what would it have cost him to take the throne through broken promises? He'd have spent those same years as a king who knew he got there through betrayal of his word. Living every day as someone he didn't recognize. Building a reign on a foundation of compromise.

Which cost is actually higher?

When you're facing your choice, count both sides. Yes, doing right will cost you. But what does doing wrong cost? Not in abstract moral terms, but in concrete reality: who do you become? What do you lose that you can never get back?

Most people focus only on what integrity will cost them. They don't calculate what compromise will cost. And compromise always costs more than you think - it costs you yourself.

Understand that the first compromise is the hardest

If Michael stays silent on this story, the next compromise will be easier. Not because the second story matters less, but because he's already established that truth has limits. He's already proven to himself that he'll stay silent when the stakes are high enough.

The tenth compromise will be automatic. The hundredth won't even register as a choice.

This is how integrity dies - not in one dramatic betrayal, but in a thousand small concessions, each individually justifiable, each slightly easier than the last.

Rama knew this. He could have told himself "I'll compromise this once, but never again." But he understood that the first compromise creates the pattern. Once you've proven you'll break your word when it's costly enough, you become someone whose word can be broken. The question becomes "how costly?" not "will I keep my word?"

The first time you compromise is the most important choice you'll ever make. Because it establishes who you are. Every subsequent compromise will reference back to that first one: "I've done it before, so I might as well be consistent."

This is why Rama's response to the first test matters so much. He established, in that moment, that he was someone who kept his word regardless of cost. Every subsequent test became easier because he knew who he was.

If you compromise the first time, every subsequent test becomes harder. Because you've established that you're someone who compromises, and now you're fighting against your own precedent.

Don't expect vindication

Michael leaks the story hoping it will matter. Maybe it does. Maybe the company is held accountable, regulations are enforced, the water is cleaned up. Maybe his sacrifice achieves something.

Or maybe the company's lawyers bury the story. Maybe the PR campaign destroys his credibility. Maybe nothing changes except that he's unemployed.

Rama didn't know he'd eventually become king when he walked into exile. He made the choice not knowing the ending. He gave up everything with no guarantee it would matter.

This is the hardest part of Rama's teaching: you don't get to know the outcome before you choose. You don't get to maintain integrity only when you're confident it will work out.

You choose integrity because of who you are, not because of what you'll get. You keep your word because you're someone who keeps their word, not because keeping your word produces good results.

Sometimes it does produce good results. Sometimes doing right changes things, earns respect, opens unexpected doors. Sometimes the cost you feared doesn't materialize the way you thought.

But sometimes it doesn't. Sometimes you pay everything and accomplish nothing except becoming someone who paid everything. That has to be enough. Because if you're only willing to maintain integrity when you're guaranteed it will work out, you don't have integrity - you have calculation.

Remember that outcomes aren't yours to control

Michael can control one thing: whether he tells the truth. He cannot control whether it changes anything. Whether the company is held accountable. Whether his sacrifice matters. Whether anything improves.

Those outcomes depend on lawyers, judges, politicians, public opinion, corporate power, economic systems, forces far beyond one journalist's decision.

Rama could control whether he kept his father's word. He could not control whether the kingdom fell into chaos, whether Bharat became a good king, whether the fourteen years mattered.

This is the liberation in Rama's teaching: you're responsible for your character, not for outcomes. You're responsible for being who you say you are, not for whether being that person achieves what you hope.

If Michael tells the truth and nothing changes - he still did his job. He was still a journalist. The failure isn't his; it's the system's. He can live with having done what was his to do, even if forces beyond him prevented it from mattering the way he hoped.

But if he stays silent, the failure is his. Because the one thing he controlled - his own integrity - he surrendered to protect outcomes he doesn't actually control anyway.

Be prepared to do it again.

The Agnipariksha teaches this. Rama's integrity wasn't tested once. It was tested repeatedly. The exile. Then Sita's trial. Each time he had to choose what mattered most. Each time it cost him.

Your test won't be once either. If you choose integrity this time, you'll face another test. And another. Each one potentially costing you. Each one asking if you meant it the first time.

This is exhausting to contemplate. But it's also clarifying. You're not trying to pass one test perfectly so you never have to face another. You're building a life where integrity is your default, even when it keeps costing you.

Michael leaks this story. Maybe six months from now, he faces another choice. And another. Each time he'll have to decide again who he is. The first choice doesn't exempt him from future ones.

But the first choice does make future ones clearer. Because he's established who he is. He's someone who tells the truth when it costs him everything. That person doesn't deliberate much when the next test comes. He knows who he is.

Accept what you cannot control - including the pain

The Agnipariksha shows us that even when you choose integrity, even when you do what you believe is right, people get hurt. Relationships suffer. Things break that you wish hadn't broken.

Rama did what he thought was right. Sita suffered for it. Some say their marriage was never the same. Was he wrong to ask for the trial? Was he right? The story doesn't tell us because maybe there was no fully right answer.

This is what makes integrity so hard. It's not just that it costs you. It's that your choice sometimes costs others. Your integrity might hurt people you love. Your principles might create collateral damage.

Michael's wife Jennifer is going to pay for his choice. His colleagues will lose jobs when the paper folds. His parents will suffer watching their son destroy his life. These are real costs to real people who don't deserve them.

He can't fix that. He can only make his choice and live with all the consequences - including the ones that hurt people he cares about.

Rama's example doesn't erase that pain. It says: sometimes integrity demands everything, including accepting that doing right creates costs you wish you could prevent. You don't get to control all the consequences. You get to control whether you're who you say you are.

That has to be enough. Because it's all you get.

What Rama Cannot Do

Rama gives us something essential: the unwavering commitment to doing what's right regardless of cost. The clarity to know your principles and the courage to uphold them when tested. The integrity to be who you say you are even when being someone else would be easier.

But sit with Michael's dilemma a little longer, and you start to see the edges of what Rama's example can't quite solve.

Michael leaks the story. He chooses integrity over survival. He becomes the journalist who stood for truth when it cost everything. Rama would be proud.

And then.

The company he exposed has unlimited legal resources. They sue him into bankruptcy. They launch a PR campaign painting him as a disgruntled employee with an agenda. They use their political connections to discredit the story. The environmental poisoning continues because one journalist's integrity, however noble, isn't enough to dismantle a system protected by money, power, and institutional support.

Michael maintained his integrity. But the problem persists. The water is still poisoned. The children are still at risk. And Michael is unemployed, possibly unemployable, his family's life upended.

Was choosing integrity wrong? No. Was it enough? Also no.

This is what Rama's story, for all its power, cannot fully address: what do you do when the right choice is unclear? When doing right in one dimension means failing in another? When your personal integrity, however uncompromising, cannot fix systemic problems that require collective action, strategic thinking, and navigating complexity that has no clean answer?

The Agnipariksha showed us this limitation. Rama chose what he thought was right - honoring public duty, addressing legitimate concerns about legitimacy. But that choice caused deep pain. It satisfied one form of righteousness while violating another. Was he right?

Was he wrong? The story doesn't give us certainty because the situation didn't allow for it.

Michael faces this too. If he stays silent, he fails his integrity. If he speaks and loses everything but nothing changes, has he succeeded? If he speaks and the newspaper folds and hundreds of people lose their jobs and the city loses its only watchdog and corruption actually gets worse - was choosing integrity the right choice?

You need something Rama's clarity doesn't provide. You need wisdom for situations where doing right isn't obvious. Where competing goods conflict. Where every option has moral weight on multiple sides. Where integrity alone cannot tell you which path honors the most important values when you cannot honor them all.

You need the wisdom of Krishna - who navigated impossible dilemmas where *dharma* itself seemed to conflict with *dharma*. Who understood that some situations are too complex for simple righteous action to solve.

And there's another limitation.

Suppose Michael chooses integrity. Suppose he speaks the truth. Suppose the story actually works - the company is held accountable, regulations are enforced, the water is cleaned up. Suppose his integrity costs him everything but achieves something meaningful.

He's still unemployed. His marriage is still strained. He's still waking up at 3am wondering if he did the right thing, if the cost was worth it, if he should have found another way. He did the right thing, but he's not at peace.

Integrity doesn't heal the anxiety. It doesn't address the addiction to validation, to success, to proving yourself. It doesn't solve the restlessness that makes you check your phone a hundred times a day hoping for vindication. It doesn't stop the voice that says you destroyed your life for nothing.

You need something else. Not instead of integrity, but alongside it. The wisdom to let go of outcomes you cannot control. To find peace even when doing right doesn't produce the results you hoped for. To be whole even when integrity costs you everything and doesn't fix what you hoped it would fix.

You need what Buddha understood - that doing right is necessary, but attachment to the results of doing right will destroy you. That inner peace isn't the reward for being righteous; it's the foundation that makes sustainable righteousness possible.

And perhaps most importantly: what if the entire system Michael is trying to expose with his one story is just a symptom? What if newspapers are dying, corporations have unlimited power to evade accountability, and individual acts of integrity cannot fix structural problems because the whole apparatus is designed to absorb, deflect, and continue regardless of individual heroes?

Then you need something even Rama's unwavering *dharma* cannot provide. You need the force of radical transformation. The avatar who comes not to preserve the world but to remake it.

You need Kalki - the one who understands that sometimes the most righteous act is not maintaining your integrity within a corrupt system, but dismantling the system so integrity becomes possible for everyone.

* * *

8

Krishna - When There Is No Right Answer

Rachel sits at her kitchen table at 2am, looking at two letters.

The first letter is from Boston Children's Hospital. Her daughter Emma, age twelve, has been accepted into their experimental treatment program for her rare autoimmune disorder. The condition is manageable now with medication, but it's progressive. Without this treatment, Emma will likely face serious complications within five years - organ damage, possibly kidney failure. The program is cutting-edge, shown remarkable results in early trials, and might give Emma a normal life.

The cost: $180,000 over two years. Insurance covers some, but her out-of-pocket will be $85,000. They'd need to relocate to Boston for the duration. Rachel would have to leave her job or work remotely at reduced pay.

The second letter is from Berklee College of Music. Her son Daniel, age seventeen, has been accepted with a partial scholarship to their performance program. Daniel is extraordinarily gifted - the kind of talent that comes along once in a generation, according to every music teacher he's had. He's been working toward this since he was seven. This is the program that could launch a real career, that could give him the life he's dreamed of.

The cost: $45,000 per year after scholarship. Four years, $180,000 total. He'd need to start in September - seven months from now.

Rachel and her husband Tom have $100,000 saved. That's it. No family money to draw from. No inheritance coming. They've already looked at loans - they could maybe borrow another $50,000, but that's pushing their debt capacity to the limit given their mortgage and Tom's income.

Do the math: they can afford one. Not both.

Emma's treatment: $85,000. Daniel's education: $180,000 over four years, starting soon. Total need: $265,000. Total available: $150,000 if they stretch everything.

They've spent three weeks running numbers, looking for solutions. Can they do Emma's treatment first, then Daniel's college later? No - he'd miss his window, lose the scholarship, probably lose the momentum of his development at this crucial age. Can they do partial treatment for Emma? The doctors say it's all or nothing - the protocol requires the full course. Can Daniel go to a cheaper school? Yes, but not one with this level of training, faculty, connections. He'd be good, but he wouldn't become what he could become.

Can they take out more loans? They've asked. The answer is no - their debt-to-income ratio is already at the limit. Can they sell their house? They'd net maybe $60,000 after paying off the mortgage, and then they'd need to rent somewhere, probably for more than their current mortgage, and where would they live during Emma's treatment in Boston?

Every option is a version of: choose one child's future over the other's.

If they choose Emma's treatment, Daniel loses Berklee. He could go to state school, study music, maybe still have a career. But everyone who knows his talent says this is the moment - Berklee, with these teachers, at this age. Miss it and he'll always wonder what he could have been. He'll know his parents chose his sister's health over his dreams. He won't say it's wrong - how could he? His sister's health obviously matters more than his education. But he'll know. And part of him will resent it forever, even though he'll hate himself for resenting it.

If they choose Daniel's education, Emma gets standard care instead of the experimental treatment. She'll probably be okay for a few years. Maybe something else will come along. Maybe they'll have more money later. Maybe it won't progress as fast as the doctors fear. But maybe it will. And if it does, if she's facing organ damage at seventeen when they could have prevented it at twelve, how does Rachel look at her and explain that they chose her brother's music career over her health?

There is no right answer. There is no clever solution they haven't found yet. There is no compromise that serves both children adequately.

Both needs are real. Both children deserve their parents' full support. Both futures matter. Both losses would be devastating.

Rachel has Rama's integrity - she wants to do right by helping both her children. But integrity doesn't tell her which child to choose. She has Matsya's discernment - she can see clearly what each choice costs. But clarity doesn't make the choice easier. She has Varaha's willingness to rescue - she wants to save both. But wanting doesn't create resources that don't exist.

This is the crisis that none of the previous avatars fully prepared her for. Not a choice between right and wrong, but a choice between two rights that cannot coexist. Not a moral failure to avoid, but an impossible situation to navigate. Not a clear principle to uphold, but competing values that demand she fail one to honor the other.

Tom sits across from her, equally exhausted. They've had this conversation every night for three weeks. They circle the same terrain, hoping for an answer that isn't there.

"What would you do?" Rachel asks, though they've asked each other this a hundred times.

"I don't know," Tom says. "If I choose Emma's health, I feel like I'm destroying Daniel's future. If I choose Daniel's dreams, I feel like I'm gambling with Emma's health. Either way, I'm failing one of them."

"Maybe we flip a coin," Rachel says, half-joking, half-serious. "At least then it wouldn't be our choice."

But it is their choice. It has to be. And they have to make it soon - Emma's treatment program starts in eight weeks. Daniel needs to confirm his enrollment in six weeks or lose his spot.

Two letters. Two children. One impossible choice.

This is the kind of dilemma that breaks people. Not because they're weak, but because there is genuinely no right answer. Just competing goods, limited resources, and the terrible necessity of choosing.

This is the crisis millions of parents face in different forms. Not grand ethical dilemmas, but grinding impossible choices. The single mother choosing between working overtime to pay rent and being home for her kids. The father choosing between caring for his aging parent and being present for his children's childhood. The parents choosing which child gets the limited resource - the medical care, the education, the opportunity, the attention.

We've learned that we need principles, stability, protection, resistance, humility, reform, and integrity. But what happens when all those things don't resolve the dilemma? When you can do right by everyone you love because doing right by one means failing another?

We need what the ancient world called Krishna.

The one who navigated impossible situations. Who counseled action even in moral ambiguity. Who understood that sometimes wisdom isn't choosing right over wrong - it's choosing which version of right you can live with when you cannot honor them all.

The Crisis of Impossible Choices

Rachel's dilemma isn't unique. It's the story playing out in millions of lives, across every dimension of human existence.

The refugee family at the border. They fled violence, traveled thousands of miles, risked everything to reach safety. Now they face a choice: attempt illegal entry and risk detention, separation, deportation - or return to the place where their lives are threatened. Stay together in danger, or separate for a chance at safety. Both choices could destroy their family. Neither is "right."

The doctor in the emergency room when ambulances arrive simultaneously. Two patients in critical condition. One is a child, the other is a parent of three young children. Both will die without immediate intervention. The doctor has capacity to save one. Not a choice between saving someone and not saving someone. A choice between which life to save when both lives are equally valuable, equally loved, equally deserving.

The climate scientist who's calculated that her research institution's funding comes partially from fossil fuel companies. Quit on principle and lose her platform, her lab, her ability to do the research that might help solve the crisis? Or stay and compromise her integrity while doing work that might actually matter? Pure principles or practical impact. She can't have both.

The manager who has to lay off 30% of her team to keep the company solvent. Every person she fires has a family depending on them. But if she doesn't make the cuts, the whole company fails and everyone loses their job. Choose which families to devastate, or choose to devastate all the families. Fire people or fire everyone. Both choices create real suffering for real people.

The social worker with a caseload of forty families and time to adequately serve twenty. Every hour she spends with one family is an hour another family doesn't get. She's not choosing between helping and not helping. She's choosing which children get the support they desperately need and which children get the minimum while she hopes they survive.

This is different from the crises we've faced before.

Rama taught us integrity - do what's right even when it costs everything. But what happens when "what's right" points in two opposite directions simultaneously? When integrity demands you honor both your children equally, but resources make that impossible?

We've learned to build inner stability, to confront corruption, to maintain our principles even when tested. All essential wisdom. But none of it resolves Rachel's dilemma.

And modern life is full of these situations.

The previous avatars helped us develop the capacity to face challenges. But they all assumed that with enough clarity, courage, integrity, and persistence, you could find the right answer. They assumed that wisdom would show you the path, even if walking it was hard.

Krishna is different. Krishna's wisdom is for situations where there is no right path. Where every option violates something sacred. The wisdom to act in moral ambiguity. To make impossible choices with full awareness of their cost. To live with the consequences of decisions where every option creates harm. To find clarity not about what's right, but about how to choose when nothing is fully right.

Thousands of years ago, in a story that still echoes today, a warrior faced a choice that made Rachel's dilemma look simple.

He had to choose whether to fight a war that was just but would require killing his own family. Where his duty to righteousness demanded he fight, and his duty to his kin demanded he refuse. Where both paths violated sacred obligations and there was genuinely no answer that honored all that mattered.

His name was Arjun. And the one who counseled him through that impossible moment was Krishna.

The one who understood that wisdom isn't always about finding the right answer. Sometimes it's about choosing with clarity when there is no right answer at all.

The Warrior Who Couldn't Fight

On the battlefield of Kurukshetra, Arjun stood between two armies and faced an impossible choice.

He was one of the greatest warriors who ever lived. Skilled with every weapon, disciplined in every practice, bound by duty to fight for righteousness. The war he was about to fight was just - his cousins, the Kauravas, had stolen his family's kingdom through deceit, refused every peaceful solution, persecuted the innocent, violated every principle of *dharma*. This wasn't a war of conquest or greed. This was a war to restore justice, to defend the oppressed, to uphold what was right.

Everything Rama stood for - integrity, duty, righteous conduct - demanded that Arjun fight.

But there was one problem.

As Arjun looked across the battlefield at the army he was supposed to destroy, he saw his grandfather Bhishma, who had taught him to hold a sword. His teacher Drona, who had trained him since childhood. His cousins, who he'd grown up with. His uncles, his kinsmen, people he loved.

Yes, they had done wrong. Yes, they deserved to face consequences. Yes, the war was just.

But to establish justice, he would have to kill his own family.

Arjun's hands began to shake. His bow felt impossibly heavy. He turned to his charioteer - Krishna, who was also his friend, his guide, his counselor.

"I can't do this," Arjun said. "Look at them. My grandfather. My teacher. People I love. How can I kill them? Even if we win, even if we restore the kingdom, even if justice is served - I'll have murdered my family to get there. How is that *dharma*? How is that right?"

"But if I don't fight," Arjun continued, "I abandon my duty. I let injustice stand. I betray my brothers who depend on me. I fail everyone who's counting on this war to restore what was stolen. I become a coward who chose comfort over righteousness."

He sat down in his chariot, overcome. "Tell me, Krishna - what should I do? If I fight, I violate my duty to my kin. If I don't fight, I violate my duty to justice. Both choices are wrong. Both paths lead to terrible consequences. There is no answer here that doesn't destroy something sacred."

This is the moment when Krishna spoke the words that became *The Bhagavad Gita* - one of the most important philosophical texts in human history. Not a sermon about easy answers, but wisdom for impossible situations.

Krishna's Counsel

Krishna didn't tell Arjun the dilemma was simple. He didn't pretend there was a clever solution that would honor all duties. He didn't offer false comfort that everything would work out fine.

Instead, he told Arjun several crucial truths.

First: "You're right that this choice is terrible. Both paths violate sacred obligations. Welcome to the human condition. This is what moral life actually looks like - not clean choices between good and evil, but agonizing choices between competing goods that can't all be honored."

Second: "But refusing to choose is still a choice. Paralysis doesn't exempt you from consequences. If you don't fight, the war still happens - your brothers still fight, probably lose without you, and injustice still prevails. You don't get neutrality. You only get to choose which failure you participate in."

Third, and most important: "Your duty - your *dharma* - is to act according to your nature and role, then release attachment to the outcome. You're a warrior. Your role in this moment is to fight for justice. That's your *dharma*. Not because it's clean or comfortable, but because it's what this situation demands of someone with your capacity and position."

"But Krishna," Arjun protested, "if I fight, I kill people I love. How can that be *dharma*?"

"Because *dharma* isn't about avoiding all harm," Krishna said. "In a broken world, sometimes all available actions cause harm. *Dharma* is about acting according to your duty and role, with full awareness of the consequences, and releasing your attachment to controlling outcomes you cannot control."

Krishna continued: "You're suffering because you want to control things that aren't yours to control. You want there to be a choice that keeps everyone alive, that honors all duties, that makes you feel good about yourself. But that choice doesn't exist. The war will be fought whether you fight or not. People will die whether you kill them or someone else does. Injustice will have consequences whether you participate in delivering those consequences or not."

"What you can control is this: Do you act according to your *dharma* - your duty as a warrior, as a brother, as someone with the capacity to fight for justice? Or do you abandon your *dharma* because fulfilling it is painful?"

"If you fight with full awareness - knowing the cost, accepting the tragedy, releasing your attachment to being the hero who saves everyone - you're acting in integrity with your role. If you refuse to fight because you want to avoid guilt, you're acting from ego and fear."

This is the heart of Krishna's wisdom, and it's deeply unsettling.

He's not saying "do whatever feels right." He's not saying "the ends justify the means." He's not offering moral relativism or convenient justifications.

He's saying: Sometimes you face situations where every option violates something sacred. Your wisdom in that moment isn't finding the perfect option - it's understanding your *dharma*, acting according to it with full awareness of the cost, and releasing your attachment to outcomes you cannot control.

The Choice

Arjun listened. He understood. It didn't make the choice easier, but it made it possible.

He picked up his bow. Not because he wanted to kill his family, but because his *dharma* - his duty, his role, his capacity - demanded he fight for justice even though it would cost him people he loved.

He fought. He won. Justice was restored. And yes, his grandfather died. His teacher died. His cousins died. The cost was exactly as terrible as he'd feared.

But he had acted according to his *dharma*. He had done what the situation demanded of someone with his capacity and role. He had made the impossible choice with full awareness of its consequences.

And this, Krishna taught, is what wisdom looks like when there is no right answer. Not avoiding the choice. Not pretending it's simple. Not achieving some perfect outcome where everyone wins.

Just acting according to your *dharma*, with full awareness, and accepting that sometimes doing your duty means causing harm you cannot prevent.

What Krishna Understood

Krishna's wisdom is harder than Rama's. Rama could give up his kingdom and know he'd done right. It was painful, but it was clear.

Arjun couldn't know he'd done right. He could only know he'd done his duty - even though it violated other sacred obligations. There was no moral clarity. No clean conscience. Just the terrible necessity of choosing when all choices cause harm.

This is the wisdom Rachel needs. Not "here's the right answer." But "here's how you choose when there is no right answer."

Your *dharma* - your duty, your role, your capacity - points to a choice. Maybe it's choosing the child whose need is more urgent. Maybe it's choosing the child whose opportunity is more time-sensitive. Maybe it's some other calculation based on your values and judgment.

But you don't get to avoid choosing. You don't get the comfort of a perfect solution. You don't get to escape the guilt of failing one child to help another.

When No Choice Is Right

Rachel is going to choose Emma.

She's known it for three days, though she's been fighting the knowledge. Trying to find another answer. Running the numbers again. Looking for the solution that lets her help both children. But the math doesn't change, and the deadline is tomorrow.

Emma's treatment. Not Daniel's education.

She hasn't told Tom yet. She hasn't told the children. She's sitting at the kitchen table at 2am because she can't sleep, because the decision is made but she can't accept it, because choosing feels like failing even though not choosing would be worse.

Here's what she knows: Emma's condition is progressive. Without treatment, she faces serious complications within five years. With treatment, she has a chance at a normal life. This is medical necessity.

Daniel's music is extraordinary. But it's not life or death. He can go to state school. He can still play, still perform, still have a career. It won't be Berklee, won't be what he's dreamed of, won't be what his talent deserves. But he'll survive.

That's the calculation. Health over dreams. Necessity over opportunity. The child whose body is failing over the child whose future is exceptional.

It sounds rational when she puts it that way. It sounds like the obvious choice.

Except Daniel has been working toward this since he was seven. Ten years of practice, of lessons, of sacrifice. He's turned down social events to rehearse. He's spent every summer at music camp instead of hanging out with friends. He's built his entire identity around this path, this dream, this moment.

And now his mother is going to tell him: sorry, your sister needs the money more. Your decade of work, your exceptional talent, your one shot at the program that could launch your career - none of it matters as much as Emma's health.

He won't say it's wrong. How could he? His sister's health obviously matters more than his education. But he'll know. He'll know his parents chose her over him. And part of him will resent it forever, even though he'll hate himself for resenting it.

Rachel knows this. She's choosing it anyway. Because the alternative is worse.

What Arjuna Faced

On the battlefield at Kurukshetra, Arjuna faced the same impossible math.

His grandfather Bhishma taught him to hold a sword. His teacher Drona trained him since childhood. His cousins, despite their corruption, were still family. Killing them to restore justice meant destroying the people who made him who he was.

But not fighting meant abandoning his brothers, betraying the oppressed, letting injustice stand. Both choices violated sacred obligations. Both paths led to terrible consequences.

Krishna didn't tell Arjuna the choice was simple. He told him: "You're right that this is terrible. Both options violate something sacred. Welcome to the human condition."

This is what Rachel needs to hear. Not that she's missing something, not that she's failing to find the right answer. But that there is no right answer. The situation itself is impossible. Her wisdom isn't finding a solution that doesn't exist - it's choosing between two goods that cannot coexist.

The Choice No One Can Make for You

Tom walks into the kitchen. It's 2:30am now. He can't sleep either.

"You've decided," he says. Not a question.

"Emma," Rachel says. "We do Emma's treatment."

Tom nods. He's been running the same calculations, reaching the same conclusion. "Daniel is going to be devastated."

"I know."

"We're taking away the thing he's worked for his entire life."

"I know."

"He might never forgive us."

"I know." Rachel's voice breaks. "But if we choose Daniel and Emma gets worse - if she's facing organ damage at seventeen when we could have prevented it at twelve - how do I look at her? How do I tell her we chose her brother's music career over her health?"

This is the agony Arjuna felt. Not uncertainty about what to do, but certainty about what it will cost. Both options clear. Both costs unbearable. Having to choose anyway.

Krishna told Arjuna: "Refusing to choose is still a choice. If you don't fight, the war still happens. You don't get neutrality. You only get to choose which failure you participate in."

If Rachel doesn't choose, both opportunities disappear. Emma misses her treatment window. Daniel loses his scholarship. Paralysis doesn't avoid consequences - it guarantees the worst version of them.

Acting According to Your *Dharma*

"What if we're wrong?" Tom asks. "What if some new treatment comes out in three years that would have worked just as well, and we destroyed Daniel's future for nothing?"

"Or what if Emma's condition progresses faster than expected," Rachel says, "and we gambled with her health for Daniel's dreams and lost?"

This is what keeps them both awake. Not just the choice, but the knowledge that they might choose wrong. That hindsight might reveal they made the terrible decision that didn't even accomplish what they hoped.

Krishna told Arjuna: "You cannot control the outcome. You can only control the integrity of your decision-making. Act according to your *dharma* - your duty, your role - and release your attachment to knowing whether you were right."

Rachel's *dharma* - her duty as a mother, her judgment about responsibility - points toward Emma's health. Not because it's certainly right, but because treating a progressive disease feels more foundational than preserving an exceptional opportunity. That's her best judgment given impossible options.

She might be wrong. Emma's treatment might not work. Daniel's resentment might damage their relationship permanently. The choice might haunt her for the rest of her life.

But not choosing would haunt her differently. And worse.

The Conversation

Three days later, Rachel and Tom sit down with Daniel.

He knows something is wrong. He's seen them whispering, seen the strain. He's seventeen - not stupid.

"We can't afford Berklee," Rachel says. "We're doing Emma's treatment instead."

Daniel's face doesn't change. He just nods. "Okay."

"Danny, I'm so sorry. Your talent, your work, everything you've dreamed of-"

"Emma's sick," Daniel says. His voice is flat. "She needs treatment. I get it. It's fine."

"It's not fine," Tom says. "Don't pretend it's fine."

"What do you want me to say?" Daniel's voice cracks. "That I'm angry Emma's sick? That I wish she'd die so I could go to music school? Of course I don't want that. Of course her health matters more. But you're taking away everything I've worked for. Ten years. And I'm supposed to just... what? Be okay with it?"

"No," Rachel says. "You're not supposed to be okay with it. This is terrible. We're failing you. I know that."

"Then why are you doing it?"

"Because failing you this way is something I can live with," Rachel says. "Failing Emma the other way - I can't. I'm so sorry."

Daniel leaves the room. They hear his door slam. They hear, faintly, him playing his instrument - the thing he does when he's upset, when words aren't enough.

Rachel starts crying. Tom holds her. This is what choosing looks like. Not clarity. Not peace. Just the awful necessity of deciding between children you love equally, knowing that whatever you choose will cause harm you cannot prevent.

What Krishna Teaches

Arjuna fought the war. He killed his grandfather, his teacher, his cousins. Justice was restored. And he carried the weight of those deaths for the rest of his life.

Krishna didn't promise him he'd feel good about his choice. Didn't promise the grief would end. Didn't promise he wouldn't wake up at 3am wondering if there was another way.

Krishna promised only this: if you act according to your *dharma* with full awareness of the cost, you can live with having done it. Not because it doesn't hurt. But because you did your best with impossible options, and that has to be enough.

Rachel chose Emma. Daniel will go to state school instead of Berklee. He'll still play music, still perform, still maybe have a career. But he'll always wonder what he could have been. And Rachel will carry that knowledge - that she had the power to give him his dream and chose not to.

She'll also carry the knowledge that she did what her judgment told her was right. That she protected the child whose need was more urgent. That she made the best choice she could with terrible options.

Both of these things are true. The choice was necessary. The choice caused real harm. She acted according to her *dharma*. She failed her son.

This is what Krishna teaches that's so much harder than Rama's clarity. Rama could give up his kingdom and know he'd done right. It hurt, but it was clear.

Rachel can't know she did right. She can only know she did her duty as she understood it. The outcome might prove her wrong. Daniel's resentment might never heal. Emma's treatment might not work.

Or it might work. Daniel might find a different path that turns out better. The choice might, in hindsight, look obviously right.

Rachel won't know for years. Maybe never. And she has to live with that uncertainty. Has to make the choice and release her attachment to knowing whether she chose correctly.

That's the wisdom Krishna offers. Not comfort. Not certainty. Just the strength to act when action requires causing harm, and the permission to be human - to do your best and live with having done it, even when your best wasn't enough to prevent suffering.

What Krishna Would Do Today

So you're facing your own impossible choice. Your own situation where every option violates something sacred. Your own moment where you have to decide knowing that whatever you choose will cause harm you cannot prevent.

What does Krishna's wisdom actually offer you?

Not a decision-making framework. Not steps to find the right answer. Something harder and more honest than that.

Stop looking for the answer that doesn't exist.

You've been running the numbers for weeks. Analyzing every angle. Hoping that if you just think about it one more time, you'll see the solution you've been missing.

You won't. Because it's not there.

This is the first and hardest teaching: some situations genuinely have no right answer. Not "no easy answer" - no right answer at all. Every option violates something you hold sacred. The resource constraint is real. The dilemma is genuine.

Your wisdom isn't finding a clever solution. It's accepting that you're choosing between competing goods that cannot both be honored.

Rachel kept looking for a way to afford both children's needs. She ran the numbers a hundred different ways. But $265,000 needed and $150,000 available doesn't become solvable through better calculation. The math is what it is.

Arjuna kept looking for a way to restore justice without killing his family. But the Kauravas wouldn't surrender peacefully, his brothers needed him to fight, and wanting there to be a third option didn't create one.

When you're facing an impossible choice, the first step is accepting it's impossible. Not as failure, but as the situation. You're not failing to find the right answer - you're facing a situation that has no right answer.

Stop torturing yourself looking for what isn't there. Start grappling with the choice between imperfect options.

Understand that paralysis is still a choice - and usually the worst one.

When every option is terrible, the temptation is to not choose. To wait. To hope something changes. To avoid being responsible for the harm your choice will cause.

But Krishna's second teaching is uncompromising: refusing to choose is still a choice. And usually it's the choice with the worst consequences.

If Rachel doesn't decide, Emma misses her treatment window and Daniel loses his scholarship. Her paralysis doesn't prevent harm - it guarantees both children lose what they need.

If Arjuna doesn't fight, the war still happens. His brothers fight without him, probably lose, injustice prevails, people die anyway. His refusal to participate doesn't create a better outcome - it just means he abandoned his duty while everything terrible happened anyway.

You don't get neutrality. You don't get to avoid responsibility by not deciding. The consequences of your paralysis are still your consequences.

This is brutal. But it's liberating too. Because it means: if you're going to cause harm anyway (through choosing or through not choosing), you might as well choose according to your best judgment rather than let circumstances choose for you.

Act according to your *dharma*, not according to outcomes you cannot control.

Here's where Krishna's wisdom gets specific and difficult.

He doesn't tell you to choose based on which outcome you prefer. He tells you to choose based on your *dharma* - your duty, your role, your understanding of responsibility given who you are and what this situation demands.

For Arjuna, his *dharma* was clear: he was a warrior, fighting for justice against real oppression. His duty was to fight, regardless of the personal cost. Not because fighting would produce perfect results, but because that was his role in that situation.

For Rachel, her *dharma* pointed toward Emma's health being more foundational than Daniel's opportunity. Not because she could predict the outcome, but because treating a progressive disease felt like more urgent necessity than preserving an exceptional education.

Your *dharma* might point differently in a similar situation. Maybe your judgment says the child's opportunity is more time-sensitive than the health issue. Maybe your values weight things differently. There's no external formula that says which is "right."

But here's the key: you choose based on your best understanding of your duty, then you release your attachment to the outcome.

Rachel chose Emma. She doesn't get to know if that was right. Emma's treatment might not work. Daniel's resentment might never heal. The whole choice might look obviously wrong in five years.

Or it might work out. Or it might work out in ways she never expected.

She can't control that. She can only control that she acted according to her best judgment of her responsibility as a mother faced with impossible options.

This is what Krishna means by "release attachment to outcomes": not that you don't care about results, but that you accept your responsibility is to act according to your *dharma*, not to guarantee good outcomes. The outcomes are influenced by forces far beyond your control.

Accept that doing right doesn't mean feeling good.

Arjuna did his duty. He fought. Justice was restored.

And he carried the grief of killing his grandfather for the rest of his life.

Krishna's wisdom doesn't promise that acting according to your *dharma* will make you feel good about yourself. It promises you can live with having acted according to your duty even when it causes terrible pain.

Rachel will wake up at 3am thinking about Daniel. She'll see him at state school and wonder what he could have been at Berklee. She'll carry the knowledge that she had the power to give him his dream and chose not to.

That grief isn't a sign she chose wrong. It's the appropriate response to having been forced into a situation where both children deserved full support and she could only fully support one.

The grief is real. So is the fact that she acted according to her best judgment. Both things are true simultaneously.

Don't expect choosing according to your *dharma* to feel clean. Expect it to hurt. Expect to grieve what you couldn't choose. Expect to wonder if you were wrong.

And know that those feelings don't mean you failed. They mean you're human, making impossible choices with real consequences for real people you love.

Don't let hindsight destroy your present judgment.

Five years from now, Rachel might have information she doesn't have now. Maybe Emma's treatment worked perfectly and she's thriving. Maybe Daniel found a different path and is actually happier. The choice might look obviously right in retrospect.

Or maybe Emma's condition progressed anyway despite treatment, and Rachel destroyed Daniel's future for nothing. The choice might look obviously wrong in retrospect.

She can't know this now. And Krishna's teaching is: you're not supposed to know the future. You're only supposed to make the best choice you can with the information and judgment you have right now.

Five years from now, Rachel might be tempted to say "I chose right" or "I chose wrong" based on how things turned out. But that's not honest. She chose according to her *dharma* with the information she had. The outcome doesn't retroactively make that choice wise or foolish - it just reveals information she didn't have access to when she decided.

This matters because it protects you from endless second-guessing. You didn't fail to predict the future correctly. You acted according to your best judgment with uncertainty. That's all you could do. That's all anyone can do.

Know the difference between impossible choices and bad choices.

Not every difficult decision is a Krishna situation.

Sometimes you're just avoiding doing what you know is right because it's costly. That's not an impossible choice - that's Rama's territory. You need integrity, not navigation of ambiguity.

Sometimes the "dilemma" is manufactured by your own ego or fear. That's not an impossible choice - that's Vamana's territory. You need humility, not complex decision-making.

Sometimes you think you have to choose between two goods but you're actually avoiding dealing with a real problem. That's not an impossible choice - that's Parashurama's territory. You need to dismantle the corrupt structure creating false dilemmas.

A real Krishna situation has specific marks:

- The competing values are genuinely sacred to you
- The resource constraint is genuinely real, not just uncomfortable
- Both options cause real harm to real people
- Refusing to choose causes worse harm than choosing
- There's no clever solution you're missing

If you're facing this - if you've checked thoroughly and this is genuinely impossible - then Krishna's wisdom applies. But don't use "it's a Krishna situation" to avoid making a hard but clear choice.

Remember that you'll face this again.

Rachel makes this choice. Maybe in five years she faces another one. Maybe she has to choose between Emma's college and Tom's aging parents' care. Maybe she has to choose between Daniel's wedding and some other pressing need.

Life will keep presenting impossible choices. This isn't a one-time test you pass and then coast.

This is exhausting. But it's also clarifying. You're not trying to make one perfect choice that resolves everything. You're building the capacity to act according to your *dharma* repeatedly, even when it keeps costing you, even when you keep causing harm you cannot prevent.

Arjuna's story doesn't end with Kurukshetra. He faced other dilemmas. Made other impossible choices. Carried other griefs.

But the first choice - the battlefield where he learned Krishna's teaching - made subsequent choices clearer. Not easier. But clearer. Because he knew who he was: someone who acts according to duty even when duty demands terrible things.

Rachel is becoming that person. Someone who makes impossible choices according to her best judgment, lives with the consequences, and doesn't let the grief of having had to choose destroy her ability to choose again when necessary.

What Krishna Cannot Do

Krishna gives us something essential: the wisdom to act when there is no right action. The clarity to choose when every choice causes harm. The strength to do our duty even when our duty demands the impossible.

But sit with Rachel's situation a little longer, and you start to see what Krishna's wisdom cannot quite solve.

Whatever choice Rachel makes, one child suffers and does not get what they deserve. Hence, Rachel still can't sleep. She still wakes up at 3am thinking. Still carries the weight of having chosen one child's future over the other's. Still wonders if there was something she didn't see, some option she missed, some way she could have helped them both.

Krishna taught her how to make the choice. But he didn't teach her how to live with having made it.

The grief doesn't stop just because you acted according to your *dharma*. The guilt doesn't disappear just because you made the best choice you could. The restless replaying of the decision doesn't cease just because the decision was necessary.

You did your duty. You chose with wisdom. You acted with integrity. And you're still suffering.

Krishna helps you make impossible choices. But making impossible choices creates wounds that Krishna's wisdom alone cannot heal.

You need something else. Not instead of Krishna's clarity, but alongside it. The wisdom to find peace with decisions that had no perfect option. To release your attachment not just to outcomes, but to the narrative that you should have been able to save everyone. To live with grief and guilt without letting them consume you.

You need what Buddha understood - that even righteous action creates suffering when action itself is entangled with impossible situations. That wisdom includes not just knowing how to act, but knowing how to be at peace when action wasn't enough.

And there's another limitation, maybe even more troubling. Rachel made her choice. But why did she face this situation in the first place?

Why does treating a child's illness cost $85,000? Why does elite music education cost $180,000? Why do parents routinely face choices between children's needs because resources are distributed so unequally that basic care and basic opportunity are luxuries most can't afford?

Krishna's wisdom helps you navigate the impossible choice with clarity and integrity. But it doesn't ask: why is this choice necessary? What would need to change so Rachel doesn't have to choose between children? What transformation of systems would make impossible dilemmas less routine?

Rachel can make the best choice available to her within the world as it is. But what about changing the world so different choices become available?

Then you need wisdom beyond Krishna's. You need the vision to see that some situations don't need better decision-making - they need dismantled systems and rebuilt structures. You need the courage to imagine and create a world where impossible choices become unnecessary.

You need Kalki - the avatar who comes not to help you navigate the broken world with grace, but to transform the brokenness itself.

Krishna's wisdom alone cannot heal the wounds that impossible choices create. Cannot address the systems that make impossible choices routine. Cannot transform the world so that acting according to your *dharma* doesn't require causing harm you cannot prevent.

* * *

9

Buddha - When You Can't Let Go

J ames sits in the third row of the elementary school auditorium, phone in his hand, watching his daughter perform in the school play.

Except he's not watching. Not really.

His eyes are on the stage where Sophie, age eight, is playing the lead role in "The Wizard of Oz" - Dorothy, the role she's practiced for three months, the role she was so excited about she could barely sleep last night. But his thumb is scrolling through his phone.

Just checking work email. Just for a second. There's a deal closing tomorrow and his boss might need him. He looks up - Sophie is singing "Somewhere Over the Rainbow." He watches for maybe ten seconds, then the phone vibrates. A text. He looks down.

It's not his boss. It's a notification that someone liked his LinkedIn post from this morning. He opens LinkedIn. While he's there, he might as well check if anyone commented. Three comments. He reads them, considers whether to respond now or later. His company's stock price notification pops up - down 2%. He opens the trading app to check. While the app loads, he switches to email. Fifteen new messages in the last ten minutes.

He looks up. Sophie is still singing, but he's missed half the song. He watches for another few seconds. The phone buzzes again. Twitter notification - someone replied to his thread about the tech industry. He opens it. Someone disagrees with his take. He feels that familiar spike of adrenaline. Should he respond? He starts typing a reply.

"Dad, are you watching?" Sophie had asked this morning. "You have to watch the whole thing, okay? Even though it's long. Promise?"

"Of course, sweetheart. I wouldn't miss it for the world."

But he's missing it. Right now. Even as he sits three rows from the stage, even as his daughter performs the role she's dreamed about, even as she searches the audience for his face - he's not there. Not really.

The email notification sounds again. He glances at the subject line. "URGENT: Client issue." His heart rate spikes. He should probably check this one. It says urgent. He opens it. It's not actually urgent - just someone cc'ing him on a thread about a meeting next week. But while he's in email, he sees another message from his boss. "Quick question about the presentation." He opens it. Reads it. Starts to respond.

He looks up. The song is over. People are clapping. Did he miss the whole thing? He claps too, not sure what just happened.

The phone buzzes. Instagram notification. His college friend posted photos from their vacation. He opens Instagram. The photos are of a beach in Thailand. He feels a pang of envy. When was the last time he took a real vacation? He scrolls through the post. 47 likes already. He considers whether to like it. While he's on Instagram, he checks his own profile. His last post - a photo from a work event - has 83 likes. Not bad, but less than his previous post. He checks who liked it, who didn't. His college roommate didn't like it. Does that mean something?

The phone buzzes again. A news alert: "Breaking: Economic data released." He opens the news app. Reads the headline. Should he adjust his portfolio? He opens the trading app again. While it loads, he switches back to email. Twenty-three new messages now.

"Dad!"

He looks up. Sophie is waving at him from the stage. The other kids are taking a bow. How long has he been on his phone? He waves back, smiling. Did he miss her whole performance?

The play continues. Sophie has another scene coming up - the one where Dorothy meets the Scarecrow. She's been practicing the lines for weeks, making James rehearse with her every night. "You have to see this part, Dad. It's the funniest one."

He puts the phone in his pocket. He's going to watch this time. He's going to be present.

His pocket buzzes. He resists for maybe thirty seconds. Then he pulls it out. Just to check what it was. Just for a second. It's a notification that his Amazon package shipped. He clicks through to tracking. Delivery scheduled for Thursday. While he's on Amazon, he sees a recommendation for a book he's been considering. He reads the reviews. Adds it to cart. Sees other recommendations. Opens a few tabs to compare prices.

He looks up. The Scarecrow scene is happening. Sophie is delivering her lines perfectly, the audience is laughing. But he missed the beginning. He watches now, phone still in his hand. His thumb unconsciously opens email again. Forty-one new messages. How has it only been twenty minutes?

After the play, in the parking lot, Sophie runs up to him, still in costume.

"Did you see me, Dad? Did you see when I sang the song? And the part with the Scarecrow?"

James hugs her. "You were amazing, sweetheart. So good."

"But did you see the part where I forgot my line but then remembered it? Mrs. Henderson said I recovered really well. Did you see that part?"

James doesn't remember. He was probably on his phone. But he can't tell her that.

"You were perfect," he says, which isn't a lie, but isn't the truth either.

In the car, Sophie talks about the performance, about what went right and what went wrong, about how nervous she was, about how the boy playing the Tin Man forgot his entrance. James says "uh-huh" and "wow" at what he hopes are the right moments, but he's not really listening. He's thinking about the client email, the LinkedIn comment, the stock price, the Amazon delivery. His phone is in the cupholder. He can see the screen lighting up with notifications. Each one feels like a tiny hook pulling his attention.

When they get home, Sophie goes to bed, still buzzing with excitement. "This was the best day ever, Dad. Thanks for coming."

James tucks her in, feeling a strange hollowness. He was there. He sat in that auditorium for ninety minutes. But was he actually there? Did he actually see his daughter's big moment, or did he watch it through a fog of email notifications and stock prices and social media updates?

He sits on the couch and opens his phone. Checks everything he already checked. Email, Twitter, LinkedIn, Instagram, news, stocks. Nothing has changed in the last ten minutes, but he checks anyway. Feels that little hit of dopamine when there's a new notification. Feels that little pit of anxiety when there isn't.

He knows this is a problem. He knows he's missing his life. He knows his daughter performed in her school play tonight and he can't actually remember most of it. He knows that when Sophie asked "did you see me?" the honest answer was no, not really, I was looking at my phone.

But even knowing this, even feeling the shame and regret, he can't stop checking. Can't stop scrolling. Can't stop chasing that next notification, that next email, that next little hit of digital stimulation that makes him feel like he's doing something important even though he's actually missing everything that matters.

He checks his phone. Nothing new. Checks again thirty seconds later. Still nothing, but he checks a third time anyway.

This is the crisis millions face today. Not dramatic addiction to substances that destroy lives obviously. But quiet addiction to digital stimulation that destroys presence, that steals attention, that makes us miss our own lives even as we're living them.

We've learned to navigate information, build stability, rescue what matters, resist tyranny, practice humility, dismantle corruption, maintain integrity, and make impossible choices. But what do we do when we can't stop? When we know something is harming us but we can't let go? When the craving is stronger than our knowledge of its cost?

We need what the ancient world called Buddha.

The prince who understood craving. Who saw how attachment creates suffering. Who found the path to freedom from the endless cycle of wanting, getting, wanting more.

The Crisis of Endless Craving

James's addiction to his phone isn't unique. It's the story playing out in billions of lives, across every form of modern existence.

The executive who can't stop working. She's at dinner with her family, but her mind is on tomorrow's presentation. She's on vacation, but she's checking email every hour. She's achieved everything she set out to achieve - the title, the salary, the respect - but it's never enough. There's always the next promotion, the next deal, the next milestone. She can't rest. Can't stop. Can't enjoy what she has because she's already chasing what she doesn't have yet.

The teenager who can't stop scrolling. He's seen every post, checked every story, refreshed every feed. There's nothing new. But he scrolls anyway. Comparing his life to everyone else's highlight reel. Feeling inadequate when others have more likes, feeling anxious when his posts don't perform, feeling empty even when they do. Each swipe promises satisfaction but delivers only the need for the next swipe.

The shopper who can't stop buying. Her closet is full of clothes she's never worn. Her garage holds exercise equipment she's never used. Her credit card debt grows every month. But when she feels stressed, sad, or empty, she opens Amazon. Each purchase promises to fill the void. Each delivery brings a moment of excitement followed immediately by hollowness. She knows buying things doesn't make her happy. She buys anyway.

The professional who can't stop achieving. He's climbed every mountain he set out to climb. Built the company. Made the money. Earned the recognition. But the satisfaction lasts maybe a day before he's restless again, looking for the next challenge, the next validation, the next proof that he matters. Success doesn't satisfy him. It just raises the bar for what counts as success.

The parent who can't stop worrying. She's checked on her children twice in the last hour. They're fine. She knows they're fine. But she checks again anyway. Scrolls through parenting forums looking for dangers she might have missed. Reads articles about every possible risk. The anxiety doesn't protect her children. It just steals her ability to enjoy them. But she can't stop.

Krishna taught us to make impossible choices. But James's problem isn't that he's facing an impossible choice. It's that he can't stop choosing his phone even when the right choice is obvious. Even when he knows he should put it down. Even when his daughter is on stage. The knowledge of what he should do doesn't translate into the ability to do it.

Rama taught us integrity - to do what's right even when it's costly. But James knows what's right. He promised Sophie he'd watch. He wants to watch. He loves her more than anything. But the craving for that next notification is stronger than his intentions. His integrity is defeated by his compulsion.

We've learned discernment, stability, courage, humility. All essential. But none of it stops the hand from reaching for the phone. None of it quiets the restless craving for more, for new, for next. None of it breaks the cycle of wanting, getting, wanting again.

Because this isn't a problem of knowledge or character or courage. It's a problem of craving itself. The fundamental human tendency to believe that satisfaction is just one more thing away - one more notification, one more achievement, one more purchase, one more scroll, one more anything.

And modern life has turned this tendency into a crisis.

We've engineered addiction into everything. Social media platforms are designed by teams of psychologists to maximize engagement - which is a polite way of saying they're designed to be addictive. Every refresh might have new content. Every notification might be important. The variable reward schedule is the same mechanism that makes slot machines so addictive, now in your pocket, available twenty-four hours a day.

Work culture glorifies busyness. "Hustle culture" treats rest as weakness and ambition as virtue. We're supposed to optimize every moment, maximize every opportunity, turn every hobby into a side hustle. The message is clear: enough is never enough. There's always another level, another goal, another version of yourself you should be becoming.

Consumer culture promises that happiness is purchasable. Every ad shows people whose lives became complete when they bought the right product. The perfect kitchen renovation, the right skincare routine, the ideal wardrobe, the latest tech. We know intellectually that things don't make us happy. But the ads keep coming, the credit cards keep working, and the packages keep arriving.

Achievement culture turns life into a competition with no finish line. College admissions that require perfection. Job markets that demand constant skill acquisition. Social comparison on steroids as everyone's accomplishments are broadcast constantly. You can never be smart enough, successful enough, accomplished enough. Because someone else is always more.

The result is a civilization of people who can't stop. Can't rest. Can't be satisfied. Can't be present. We're all addicted to something - phones, work, shopping, achievement, food, alcohol, validation, busyness itself. The specific substance varies, but the pattern is identical: craving, temporary satisfaction, return of craving, stronger need for more.

We know we're missing our lives. James knows he missed Sophie's play. The executive knows she's missing her family. The teenager knows the scrolling makes him miserable. The shopper knows the purchases don't help. We all know.

But knowing doesn't stop the craving. Understanding doesn't break the cycle. Wanting to change doesn't translate into the ability to change.

This is what makes addiction so insidious. It's not that we're ignorant or weak or lacking in willpower. It's that craving has its own momentum. Once the pattern is established - stress triggers phone checking, or emptiness triggers shopping, or anxiety triggers scrolling - the habit becomes automatic. The craving arises before conscious thought. The hand reaches for the phone before you've decided to check it.

And each time we satisfy the craving, we strengthen the pattern. Each time James checks his phone and gets a notification, his brain learns: checking brings reward. Each time the executive achieves something and feels momentarily satisfied before becoming restless again, her brain learns: satisfaction requires constant achievement. Each time the teenager scrolls and finds something interesting, his brain learns: scrolling might bring stimulation.

The cycle perpetuates itself. And we're caught in it, watching ourselves do things we don't want to do, knowing we're missing what matters, unable to stop.

James sits on his couch, checking his phone for the hundredth time tonight. He missed his daughter's play. He feels terrible about it. He's promising himself he'll do better tomorrow.

But will he? Can he?

Tomorrow there will be more emails. More notifications. More news. More updates. More things that feel urgent but aren't. More little hits of dopamine from digital stimulation. More craving for just one more check.

And unless something changes - not his intentions, not his knowledge, but something fundamental about his relationship to craving itself - he'll miss tomorrow too. And the day after. And the moments that matter will slip past while he's scrolling through moments that don't.

This is the crisis of addiction in its modern form. Not the dramatic collapse of substance abuse, though that's real too. But the quiet epidemic of craving that steals our presence, fragments our attention, and makes us strangers to our own lives even as we're living them.

We've learned to navigate complexity. But we haven't learned to stop. We've learned to make hard choices. But we haven't learned to choose rest. We've learned to act with integrity. But we haven't learned to be at peace.

We need wisdom for this. Not the wisdom to do more or try harder or achieve more. The wisdom to let go. To stop. To be satisfied. To break the cycle of craving that no amount of achieving, acquiring, or scrolling will ever truly satisfy.

The ancient world had someone who understood this. A prince who had everything anyone could want - wealth, power, pleasure, comfort - and realized that having everything meant nothing if craving never stopped.

Who walked away from it all to find the truth about suffering and satisfaction. Who discovered that freedom isn't getting what you want - it's wanting what you have. That peace isn't one more achievement away - it's available right now, if you can stop chasing long enough to find it.

His name was Siddharth. The world came to know him as Buddha - the awakened one.

The Prince Who Had Everything and Nothing

Twenty-five hundred years ago, in what is now Nepal, there lived a prince named Siddharth Gautam.

He had everything James wishes he had. Wealth beyond measure. A palace designed for pleasure. Beautiful gardens. The finest food. Musicians and dancers for entertainment. A loving wife. A newborn son. Every comfort, every luxury, every indulgence available to a human being in that time and place.

His father, the king, had worked hard to give him this life. When Siddharth was born, a prophecy said he would become either a great king or a great spiritual teacher who would renounce the world. His father, wanting him to be a king, decided to shield him from anything that might make him question the value of worldly pleasure. He built walls around the palace grounds. He filled Siddharth's life with beauty and comfort. He made sure his son never saw suffering, never encountered anything that might make him restless for something beyond pleasure and power.

For twenty-nine years, it worked. Siddharth lived in luxury, married, had a child, enjoyed every pleasure available. He was, by any external measure, living the dream.

But he was restless. Despite having everything, he felt like he had nothing. The pleasures satisfied him briefly, then left him wanting more. The comforts felt hollow. He had the sense that he was living in a beautiful prison, protected from something real that he needed to see.

One day, against his father's wishes, Siddharth left the palace grounds. What he saw changed everything.

The Four Sights

First, he saw an old man. Bent with age, struggling to walk, skin weathered and wrinkled. Siddharth had never seen old age before. He asked his charioteer, "What happened to this man?"

"He is old, my lord. This is what happens to everyone who lives long enough. You, me, everyone you love - if we don't die young, we will become like this."

Second, he saw a sick person. Ravaged by disease, in obvious pain. Again, he'd never seen illness. "Will this happen to me?" he asked.

"It can happen to anyone, my lord. No amount of wealth protects you from sickness."

Third, he saw a corpse being carried to cremation. Death, which he'd been sheltered from his entire life. "Is this everyone's fate?"

"Yes, my lord. Everyone dies. Your father, your wife, your son, you - everyone."

Fourth, he saw a wandering ascetic. A spiritual seeker who had given up worldly life to search for truth. Unlike the old man, the sick person, and the corpse, this person had peace on their face. Not happiness from pleasure, but a deep calm that seemed to come from somewhere else.

Siddharth returned to the palace understanding something he'd never known before: suffering is real. Old age, sickness, death - they come for everyone, regardless of wealth or status. And more importantly: pleasure doesn't prevent suffering. He had every pleasure available, and he was still suffering - from the restlessness, the hollowness, the sense that something was missing.

That night, he looked at his sleeping wife and son. He loved them. But he realized: if he stayed, he would spend his life trying to hold onto things that couldn't be held. Trying to prevent aging he couldn't prevent. Trying to avoid sickness and death that were inevitable. Trying to find satisfaction in pleasures that never truly satisfied.

He made an impossible choice. He left. In the middle of the night, he walked away from his palace, his family, his kingdom, everything. Not because he didn't love them, but because he needed to understand suffering and how to end it. And he knew he couldn't find that answer while continuing to chase pleasure and avoid pain.

The Search

For six years, Siddharth tried everything. He studied with the greatest spiritual teachers of his time. He practiced meditation. He learned philosophy. But the answers they offered didn't satisfy him.

Then he tried the opposite extreme. If pleasure didn't bring peace, maybe he needed to reject pleasure entirely. He became an ascetic, practicing extreme self-denial. He ate almost nothing - one grain of rice a day. He pushed his body to the edge of death. He thought that by rejecting all physical comfort, he might find spiritual truth.

It didn't work. He just became weak, his mind clouded by hunger. He realized: extreme indulgence doesn't end suffering. But extreme deprivation doesn't end it either. Both are just different forms of craving - one craving pleasure, the other craving some idealized spiritual purity.

This was his breakthrough. What if the problem wasn't pleasure or pain, comfort or discomfort, having or not having? What if the problem was the craving itself? The endless wanting more, the constant dissatisfaction, the belief that peace was somewhere else, in some other state, if only you could achieve it?

The Middle Way

Siddharth stopped his extreme fasting. He ate a normal meal. He decided to practice what he later called the Middle Way - neither indulgence nor deprivation, neither chasing pleasure nor fleeing it. Just sitting with what is, without craving for it to be different.

He sat under a tree - later called the Bodhi tree, the tree of awakening - and meditated. Not seeking anything. Not trying to achieve a special state. Just watching his mind. Watching how craving arose. Watching how it created suffering. Watching how it could be released.

For days, he sat. His mind threw everything at him - desire, fear, doubt, memories, fantasies. Every temptation to get up and do something, to achieve something, to become something other than what he was in that moment.

He just watched. Didn't fight it. Didn't indulge it. Just observed the arising and passing of wanting without acting on it.

And then something shifted. The craving released. Not because he defeated it or transcended it or became someone special. But because he saw it clearly enough that it lost its power. He understood, deep in his bones, that craving for things to be different than they are is the root of suffering. And that freedom comes not from getting what you want, but from releasing the wanting itself.

He became Buddha - the awakened one. Not because he achieved some supernatural state, but because he woke up to how suffering works and how it can end.

The Four Noble Truths

What Buddha understood, sitting under that tree, became the foundation of his teaching:

First Noble Truth: Suffering exists. Not just dramatic suffering like death and disease, but the everyday suffering of dissatisfaction, of wanting things to be different, of never quite being at peace. Even pleasure contains suffering, because pleasure fades and we crave its return.

Second Noble Truth: Craving causes suffering. Not the external circumstances of life, but our relationship to them. Our endless wanting for more, different, better. Our inability to rest with what is. Our belief that satisfaction is just one more thing away.

Third Noble Truth: Suffering can end. Not by getting everything you want - Buddha had tried that - but by releasing the craving. By finding peace with what is rather than constantly chasing what isn't.

Fourth Noble Truth: There's a path to ending suffering. Not through extreme indulgence or extreme denial, but through the Middle Way. Through awareness of how craving arises and the practice of letting it go.

What Buddha Saw

Buddha didn't discover that wanting things is bad. He discovered that the endless cycle of wanting, getting, wanting more is what keeps us suffering. That satisfaction isn't found by fulfilling every desire - there will always be another desire. It's found by breaking the cycle itself.

James on his couch, checking his phone for the hundredth time, is caught in exactly what Buddha described. Each notification promises satisfaction. Each check delivers only the craving for another check. The scrolling never ends because satisfaction isn't found in what you're scrolling toward - it's found in stopping the scroll.

The executive who can't rest isn't suffering because she hasn't achieved enough. She's suffering because achievement itself has become her craving. Each success brings momentary satisfaction followed immediately by the need for more success. Buddha would recognize this immediately: she's trying to fill a bottomless cup. The problem isn't that she needs to pour more. The problem is the cup itself.

Buddha's insight is simple and revolutionary: You don't need one more thing. You don't need to become someone else. You don't need to achieve more or acquire more or scroll more. You need to see clearly how the wanting itself creates the suffering, and learn to let it go.

Not to become someone who wants nothing - that's just another form of craving, craving for non-craving. But to be someone who can want something without being controlled by the wanting. Who can enjoy pleasure without needing it to continue. Who can face pain without needing it to end immediately. Who can be present with life as it actually is, rather than constantly reaching for life as you imagine it should be.

This is what Buddha offers James. Not a way to manage his phone usage better, but a way to break free from the craving that makes him unable to put it down even when his daughter is on stage.

Not tips and tricks. But understanding the nature of craving itself, and the path to freedom from it.

When Having Everything Means Nothing

Siddharth had wealth, comfort, love, pleasure - everything external that James is working toward. And he was miserable. Not because those things were bad, but because the having of them didn't end the wanting. Each pleasure satisfied briefly, then the craving returned. The palace was beautiful, but he was restless in it.

James has education, a good job, a home, a family he loves, a phone that connects him to the entire world. And he's on his couch at 10pm, compulsively checking notifications, unable to rest. Not because he needs more information or more connection, but because the craving to check has become stronger than his ability to choose not to.

Buddha's insight cuts to the heart of both their situations: The problem isn't what you have or don't have. The problem is that craving itself is never satisfied. You can feed it forever and it just gets hungrier.

Look at what James is actually craving. Is it the information in those emails? No - most of them aren't important. Is it the social validation from likes and comments? Partly, but getting validation doesn't end the need for more validation. Is it staying connected to work, to current events, to his social network? On the surface, yes. But deeper down, he's craving that little hit of stimulation, that promise that the next notification might be the one that finally satisfies.

It never is. It never can be. Because the satisfaction James is seeking isn't in the next notification - it's in stopping the search for the next notification.

This is what Buddha understood. Siddharth tried pleasure - it didn't work. He tried deprivation - it didn't work. He tried achievement, learning, spiritual practices. Nothing worked. Because he was trying to fill a need that couldn't be filled by external things. The craving itself was the problem.

The Cycle We're All Caught In

The executive who can't stop achieving - Buddha would recognize this immediately. She's not suffering because she hasn't achieved enough. She's suffering because she's trying to find peace through achievement, which is like trying to quench thirst by drinking salt water. Each success brings momentary relief followed by intensified craving for more.

The teenager scrolling through social media - Buddha saw this too. He's not sad because other people have better lives. He's sad because he's comparing his life to curated highlights, believing that satisfaction exists somewhere else, in some other life. The scrolling perpetuates the dissatisfaction it promises to cure.

The shopper buying things she doesn't need - Buddha understood this in his palace. The acquisition promises to fill an emptiness. The packages arrive. The emptiness remains. Because the emptiness isn't an absence of things - it's the presence of craving.

Modern life hasn't created craving - humans have always struggled with this. But modern life has made craving more intense and more inescapable. We've engineered environments that trigger craving constantly. Notifications designed to create anxiety and relief. Infinite scrolls that never end. Consumer culture that treats dissatisfaction as an opportunity for profit. Work culture that treats rest as failure.

And we've lost the practices that help people recognize and release craving. We've replaced meditation with distraction, contemplation with consumption, presence with productivity. We're training ourselves to respond to every itch with a scratch, every discomfort with a fix, every moment of boredom with stimulation.

The result is a civilization of people who've forgotten how to rest. Who mistake constant stimulation for vitality. Who believe that peace is something to achieve rather than something to discover in the midst of life as it is.

What Buddha Offers

Buddha's teaching isn't "stop wanting things." It's "see clearly how wanting works, and you can be free from being controlled by it."

James doesn't need to throw away his phone. He needs to see what he's actually doing when he picks it up during Sophie's play. He's not seeking information. He's responding to craving - that restless feeling that maybe there's something important he's missing, that maybe the next notification will matter, that maybe checking will bring relief.

If he can see the craving clearly - feel it arise, recognize what it is, watch it without immediately acting on it - he gains a choice. Not a choice between checking and suffering from not checking. A choice to let the craving pass without needing to satisfy it.

This is the Middle Way Buddha discovered. Not fighting the craving. Not indulging it. Just seeing it clearly enough that it loses its compulsive power.

The executive doesn't need to stop achieving. She needs to see that she's using achievement to fill a sense of unworthiness that achievement can never actually fill. If she can see that pattern clearly, she can achieve things because they matter, not because she's trying to prove something that can't be proven through achievement.

The teenager doesn't need to delete social media. He needs to see that he's comparing his real life to others' curated lives, and that satisfaction isn't found by making his life look better - it's found by releasing the need for his life to look any particular way.

Connecting to What Came Before

Remember Rachel from Krishna's chapter? She made her impossible choice between Emma's treatment and Daniel's education. Let's say she chose Emma. Daniel didn't get Berklee. He's at state school now.

Krishna helped Rachel make the choice. But Krishna didn't help her find peace with having made it. She still wakes up at 3am worrying about Daniel. Still wonders if she chose wrong. Still craves certainty she can't have. Still wants to control an outcome that's already determined.

Buddha offers what Krishna couldn't: the ability to release the craving for the past to be different than it was. Rachel can't change her choice. But she can stop torturing herself by replaying it endlessly. She can release her attachment to knowing for certain whether she was "right." She can find peace with having done her best even though she can't know if her best was enough.

This is what Buddha adds to everything we've learned. Rama taught integrity, Krishna taught wisdom in complexity. But both still involve doing, choosing, acting. Buddha teaches something deeper: how to be at peace with what you've done, what you couldn't do, what you can't control.

How to stop the endless cycle of wanting things to be different than they are. How to find satisfaction not in getting what you want, but in releasing the tyranny of wanting itself.

The Difficulty

This is perhaps the hardest wisdom of all. Because craving feels like life itself. The restlessness feels like ambition. The dissatisfaction feels like motivation. The endless reaching for more feels like what makes us human.

Buddha says: No. That's just suffering wearing the mask of purpose.

Real life is available right now. Real satisfaction is available right now. Not after you check one more email, achieve one more thing, buy one more product, or scroll one more feed. Right now. If you can stop reaching long enough to notice what you already have.

James sits on his couch. His daughter is asleep upstairs. He has a home, a family, a life. Everything that actually matters is here, right now.

But he can't feel it. Can't be present with it. Because he's trapped in the cycle of craving, reaching for the next notification, the next stimulation, the next momentary relief that will bring only more craving.

Buddha offers him the key to the prison he's locked himself in. Not through more achieving, but through seeing clearly enough to let go.

What Buddha Would Do Today

So what do you actually do when you're sitting on that couch, hand reaching for your phone, craving pulling you away from your life?

Buddha's wisdom offers practical guidance that's simple to understand but not easy to practice.

Notice the craving before you act on it.

This is the foundation of everything. Most of the time, the craving arises and we immediately satisfy it. Hand reaches for phone. Email opens. Scroll begins. The action happens so automatically that we barely register choosing it.

Buddha's first teaching: Create a gap between craving and action.

When you feel the urge to check your phone, pause for three seconds. Don't fight the urge. Don't tell yourself you shouldn't feel it. Just notice it. "There's the craving to check my phone." Feel where it lives in your body - the restlessness in your chest, the itch in your fingers, the anxiety that maybe you're missing something.

Three seconds. That's all. If after three seconds you still want to check, check. But create that tiny gap of awareness.

What happens in that gap is remarkable. Sometimes the craving passes on its own - you realize there's nothing you actually need to check. Sometimes you notice what you're actually feeling - bored, anxious, avoiding something uncomfortable. Sometimes you choose to check anyway, but now it's a choice rather than a compulsion.

The gap is where freedom lives.

Identify what you're really craving.

James thinks he's craving information from his emails. Buddha would ask: What are you actually craving?

Maybe it's the dopamine hit of a new notification. Maybe it's relief from the anxiety of potentially missing something. Maybe it's distraction from uncomfortable feelings. Maybe it's proof that you're important because people need you. Maybe it's escape from the present moment which feels boring or difficult.

The surface craving (check phone) usually masks a deeper craving (feel important, avoid discomfort, get stimulation). If you only address the surface level, you're treating symptoms.

Try this: When you feel the urge to check your phone, ask yourself "What am I actually hoping to feel right now?" Not what information you hope to find, but what emotional state you're seeking.

Often just identifying the real craving reduces its power. "Oh, I'm not craving news updates. I'm craving reassurance that I matter." Once you see that clearly, you can address it directly rather than through the endless proxy of checking your phone.

Practice doing nothing.

This sounds absurd in our productivity-obsessed culture. But it's essential.

Set aside five minutes a day to literally do nothing. Not meditate with a goal. Not practice mindfulness to become calmer. Just sit. Don't check your phone. Don't plan your day. Don't try to be productive. Just be.

The craving will arise. You'll want to check something, do something, achieve something. Notice it. Let it be there. Watch it arise, peak, and pass without acting on it.

This is how you learn that craving isn't an emergency. It feels urgent - like you must check the phone right now, must know the news right now, must respond to that email right now. But if you sit with it, you discover: it's just a feeling. It arises. It passes. You don't die from not satisfying it.

This practice is like lifting weights for your ability to not respond to every craving. Start with five minutes. The craving will be intense. That's normal. You're breaking a pattern your brain has strengthened for years.

Set boundaries that make space for presence.

You can't rely purely on willpower to resist craving when your environment is engineered to trigger it constantly. You need structural changes.

Not because you lack discipline. Because you're human, and humans respond to their environment.

Some practical boundaries:

- Leave your phone in another room during meals, during time with your kids, during the hour before bed
- Turn off all non-essential notifications (you don't need to know instantly when someone likes your post)
- Designate phone-free times (first hour after waking, last hour before sleep)
- Delete apps that trigger compulsive use, or set screen time limits
- Create friction - put your phone somewhere you have to consciously retrieve it rather than where it's always within arm's reach

These aren't punishments. They're compassion. You're helping yourself by removing constant triggers for craving.

When you do use technology, use it intentionally.

Buddha's Middle Way applies here. The answer isn't to throw away your phone and move to a monastery (unless you're called to that). It's to change your relationship with technology from compulsive to intentional.

Before you pick up your phone, decide what you're going to do and for how long. "I'm going to check email for ten minutes." Then do that. Then put it down.

The difference between intentional use and compulsive use isn't what you do - it's whether you're in control of it or it's in control of you.

James can use his phone. But when he's at Sophie's play, the phone stays in his pocket. Not because phones are bad, but because that moment belongs to his daughter, and he's chosen to be present for it.

Accept that you'll fail, repeatedly.

Here's what Buddha would tell James: You're going to check your phone when you shouldn't. You're going to miss moments. You're going to break your own rules. You're going to feel the craving and satisfy it automatically before you remember to pause.

This isn't failure. This is learning.

The pattern of craving and compulsion has been strengthened over years or decades. It doesn't break in a week because you learned some techniques. You're rewiring your brain, which takes time and patience.

When you check your phone during dinner even though you set a boundary against it, don't waste energy on self-judgment. Just notice: "I did it again. The craving was strong. I acted automatically." Then make the choice again for next time.

Each time you notice, you strengthen awareness. Each time you pause, even for a second, you strengthen the gap between craving and action. Each time you see clearly what you're actually craving, you weaken its unconscious control.

Progress isn't linear. Some days you'll feel free from the compulsion. Some days it'll feel overwhelming. Both are normal.

Know when you need more than self-practice.

Buddha's wisdom is profound, but some addictions require more than individual practice.

If you can't stop drinking on your own, you need support - therapy, AA, rehab, whatever works. If your phone use has become so compulsive that these practices feel impossible, you might need help - delete the apps entirely, use a basic phone, work with a therapist who specializes in technology addiction.

If your work addiction is destroying your health and you can't stop on your own, you might need to change jobs, set hard boundaries with professional help, or address underlying issues about worth and identity with a therapist.

Buddha's path is available to everyone, but not everyone can walk it alone. Knowing when you need support isn't weakness. It's wisdom.

Remember what you're doing this for.

James isn't trying to stop using his phone so he can be a better person or achieve some spiritual ideal. He's doing it because he loves his daughter and he's missing her life. Because presence matters more than notifications. Because this moment, right here, is his life - and if he spends it all craving the next moment, he'll have no life at all.

That's what Buddha saw. Life is happening now. Satisfaction is available now. Not after you check one more thing, achieve one more goal, acquire one more object. Now.

But you can only experience what's happening now if you stop reaching for what's not here and start noticing what is.

Your daughter on stage. Your family at dinner. The sunset you almost missed because you were scrolling. The conversation you weren't fully present for. The moments that vanish while you're chasing moments that never fully arrive.

Buddha offers you those moments back. Not through achieving more, but through craving less. Not through becoming someone else, but through being fully present as who you already are.

The freedom isn't one more scroll away. It's in putting down the phone and noticing what's already here.

What Buddha Cannot Do

Buddha gives us something essential: the wisdom to see craving clearly and the path to release it. The understanding that satisfaction isn't found by fulfilling every desire, but by breaking free from desire's control. The ability to be present with life as it is rather than constantly reaching for life as we wish it were.

But sit with James's situation a little longer, and you start to see what Buddha's wisdom alone cannot quite solve.

James practices. He creates the gap between craving and action. He notices when he's reaching for his phone automatically. He sets boundaries - phone stays in another room during family dinner. He does his five minutes of doing nothing each day. He's building the awareness that Buddha described.

It helps. He's more present. He catches himself before checking his phone during Sophie's bedtime story. He experiences moments of genuine rest instead of constant restlessness.

But then he goes to work.

His company uses Slack, which sends notifications constantly. His performance review is partially based on response time to messages. His boss texts at 9pm expecting answers. The entire office culture treats constant availability as professionalism and boundaries as lack of commitment.

His industry uses social media for networking and visibility. Not participating means being invisible. Not checking regularly means missing opportunities. The system requires the very behavior Buddha teaches him to release.

His phone is designed by teams of engineers whose job is to make it maximally addictive. The apps employ variable reward schedules - the same mechanism that makes slot machines so addictive. Every refresh might have something new. Every notification might be important. The technology is literally engineered to defeat the kind of awareness Buddha taught.

James can practice letting go of craving. But he's practicing in an environment designed to manufacture craving constantly.

This is the limitation Buddha cannot fully address. Buddha offers individual liberation - the path for one person to free themselves from craving. But what happens when the entire system is structured to create and exploit craving? When the economy depends on dissatisfaction? When companies profit from addiction? When culture treats constant busyness as virtue and rest as laziness?

James can find moments of peace. But the notifications keep coming. The work demands keep escalating. The social media platforms keep optimizing for engagement. The consumer culture keeps promising that satisfaction is one more purchase away.

Individual practice is necessary. But is it sufficient when the water you're swimming in is designed to drown you?

Buddha would say: You can't control the external world, only your response to it. True. But there's a difference between choosing your response to natural human craving, and choosing your response to craving that's been artificially amplified by systems designed to exploit your vulnerabilities for profit.

The executive who can't stop working isn't just dealing with her own achievement addiction. She's dealing with a work culture that ties her worth to her productivity, that measures her value by her availability, that promotes people who sacrifice health and family for career advancement.

The teenager who can't stop scrolling isn't just dealing with his own comparison tendencies. He's dealing with algorithms designed to show him content that triggers insecurity, with platforms that profit from his distress, with a social ecosystem that measures worth in likes and followers.

The shopper who can't stop buying isn't just dealing with her own emptiness. She's dealing with trillion-dollar advertising industries that study psychology to create artificial needs, with targeted ads that follow her everywhere, with an economy that requires constant consumption to function.

Buddha can teach each of them to see their craving clearly. But what about the systems that manufacture craving systematically? What about the structures that make liberation a constant struggle against overwhelming force?

Individual liberation is crucial. James needs what Buddha offers. But James also needs something more. He needs work cultures that don't require constant availability. He needs technology designed for human wellbeing instead of maximum engagement. He needs economic systems that don't depend on manufactured dissatisfaction. He needs a society that treats rest as wisdom rather than laziness.

Buddha teaches you how to swim. But what happens when the current is so strong that even good swimmers struggle to make progress? When the water itself is poisoned? When the river's course needs to change?

Then you need wisdom beyond individual practice. You need the vision to see that some problems aren't solved by better individual behavior, but by transforming the systems that create the problems. You need the courage to imagine and build structures that support human flourishing instead of exploiting human vulnerability.

You need the final avatar. The one who comes not to help individuals navigate a broken world, but to transform the brokenness itself.

Buddha is essential. James desperately needs the wisdom to release craving, to find presence, to break free from compulsion. Every executive needs this. Every teenager needs this. Every person caught in cycles of wanting needs this.

But individual liberation alone cannot transform the systems that engineer addiction, the cultures that glorify busyness, the economies that depend on dissatisfaction, the technologies designed to exploit our vulnerabilities.

For that, we need Kalki - the avatar yet to come. The one who understands that sometimes the most compassionate act isn't teaching people to swim better, but changing the direction of the river itself.

* * *

10

Kalki - When the System Itself Must Change

Ravi sits in a congressional hearing room at 11pm, alone, reviewing testimony from today's session on artificial intelligence regulation.

He's a senior policy advisor specializing in emerging technology. For three years, he's been working on frameworks to govern AI - guidelines for transparency, accountability, safety, fairness. He's helped draft legislation. He's consulted with tech companies, academics, civil society groups. He's done everything you're supposed to do when you want to regulate a transformative technology responsibly.

And sitting here tonight, reading through eight hours of testimony, he realizes: none of it is enough. Not even close.

The testimony today covered AI's impact across every domain. He's organized his notes by crisis:

Information and Truth: AI-generated deepfakes so convincing that no one can tell what's real anymore. Recommendation algorithms that don't just show you misinformation - they generate personalized misinformation designed specifically to manipulate you. Matsya taught us to navigate the flood of information, but AI is creating floods that drown any attempt at discernment.

Mental Health and Stability: AI chatbots that millions of lonely people form attachments to. Social media algorithms optimized not for connection but for engagement, which means optimized for outrage, envy, and addiction. Kurma taught us to build inner stability, but AI systems are designed to destabilize us for profit.

Environmental Destruction: Data centers consuming more electricity than entire countries. AI used to optimize extraction of every last resource. Climate models that predict catastrophe while AI accelerates the very systems causing it. Varaha taught us to rescue what's buried, but AI is helping bury the planet faster.

Concentration of Power: A handful of companies controlling technology that will reshape civilization. AI systems that amplify existing inequalities - facial recognition that works poorly on dark skin, hiring algorithms that discriminate, lending systems that deny opportunity. Narasimha taught us to resist tyranny, but AI is creating new forms of tyranny that don't need human tyrants.

Economic Inequality: Wealth concentrating in the hands of whoever controls AI. Workers displaced by automation with no plan for their futures. The gap between those who benefit from AI and those who are harmed by it growing exponentially. Vamana taught us humility about our limits, but those with AI power feel unlimited.

Institutional Corruption: Regulatory capture where the companies being regulated write the regulations. Lobbying that ensures AI development serves corporate profit over public good. Systems too complex for any oversight body to understand, let alone govern. Parashurama taught us to dismantle corruption, but AI makes corruption harder to see and easier to execute.

Impossible Choices: Parents choosing whether to give their children AI tutors that work brilliantly but collect invasive data. Doctors choosing whether to use AI diagnostics that are accurate but biased. Krishna taught us to navigate impossible choices, but AI is creating impossible choices at scale, forcing millions of people into dilemmas that shouldn't exist.

Addiction and Craving: Every app, every platform, every digital interaction optimized to keep you engaged. AI that knows your vulnerabilities better than you do and exploits them systematically. Buddha taught us to release craving, but AI is engineered to manufacture craving faster than anyone can release it.

Ravi looks at his notes. Eight crises. Eight avatars' worth of wisdom. All of it necessary. None of it sufficient.

Because here's what he's realizing: You can't regulate your way out of this.

He's tried. God knows he's tried. The legislation he's helped draft includes provisions for algorithmic transparency, impact assessments, accountability mechanisms, safety standards, anti-discrimination requirements. It's comprehensive. It's well-intentioned. It's backed by experts.

And it's inadequate.

Not because the regulations are poorly designed, but because they're trying to make an inherently harmful system slightly less harmful. They're trying to put guardrails on a vehicle that's heading toward a cliff. They're trying to govern a technology that's developing faster than any regulatory process can keep up with.

The testimony today made this clear. A tech CEO explained how his company complies with every regulation while still deploying AI systems that amplify misinformation, degrade mental health, and concentrate power. "We follow all the rules," he said, smiling. And he was telling the truth. The rules allow harm. The rules were written to allow harm, because the rules were written within a system designed to prioritize profit over people.

An AI researcher testified that the technology is advancing so rapidly that by the time regulations are finalized, they'll be regulating last year's AI while this year's AI has already created new risks no one anticipated. "You're playing catch-up with a player that's accelerating away from you," she said.

A labor organizer testified that workers displaced by AI automation need support, but the economic system treats their displacement as collateral damage rather than as a crisis demanding response. "You're trying to patch a system that's designed to sacrifice workers for efficiency," he said.

A civil rights advocate testified that AI bias isn't a bug to be fixed with better data - it's a feature of systems built in a society with structural inequality. "You can't fix biased AI without fixing the biased society that creates it," she said.

One after another, the message was the same: The problems with AI aren't technical glitches to be debugged. They're features of a system - economic, political, social - that treats technology as a tool for profit and power rather than for human flourishing.

Ravi has spent three years trying to make the system work better. Tonight, he's confronting the possibility that the system itself is the problem.

He thinks about all the wisdom we've gathered. Matsya's discernment. Kurma's stability. Varaha's protection. Narasimha's resistance. Vamana's humility. Parashurama's reform. Rama's integrity. Krishna's navigation of complexity. Buddha's release from craving.

All essential. All necessary. All insufficient if the system they're operating within is designed to create the very crises they're trying to address.

You can have perfect discernment and still be overwhelmed by AI-generated misinformation at scale. You can have inner stability and still be destabilized by algorithms optimized to hack your psychology. You can resist individual tyrants while power concentrates in systems too complex and diffuse to resist. You can maintain integrity while working in structures that make ethical action nearly impossible. You can release personal craving while swimming in environments engineered to manufacture it industrially.

The wisdom is real. The practice is real. The necessity is real.

But what happens when the water you're swimming in is poisoned? When the current is designed to drown you? When the river's course needs to change?

Ravi closes his laptop. Tomorrow there will be another hearing. More testimony. More proposed regulations that tinker at the edges while the core problems accelerate.

He's done with tinkering.

The question isn't how to regulate AI within the existing system. The question is: what system do we need to build where AI serves human flourishing rather than extracting from it? What transformation is necessary not just in technology policy, but in economic structures, power distribution, values, and priorities?

This is the crisis that all the others point toward. Not another problem to solve with wisdom and practice, but a fundamental question about the systems we've built and whether they can be reformed or need to be reimagined entirely.

We need what the ancient world called Kalki.

The avatar who comes not to help us navigate the end of an age, but to transform it. Who understands that sometimes compassion means not teaching people to swim better, but changing the course of the river itself.

The Crisis of Systems Design

Ravi's realization isn't unique. It's the awakening happening across every domain where people have been trying to fix problems only to discover that the problems are features of the system, not bugs.

The climate scientist who's spent thirty years researching solutions, publishing papers, advising governments - and watching emissions continue to rise. She's realized: the problem isn't lack of knowledge about climate change. We've known what to do for decades. The problem is an economic system that profits from the very activities destroying the planet. You can't science your way out of an economic structure designed to maximize extraction and consumption.

The healthcare worker who's dedicated his career to helping patients, only to watch the system he works in prioritize profit over care. He's realized: the problem isn't individual doctors making bad decisions. It's a healthcare system designed to generate revenue rather than health. You can't compassion your way out of a structure where denying care is more profitable than providing it.

The teacher who's spent twenty years trying to reach struggling students, watching funding decrease, class sizes increase, and standardized testing dominate. She's realized: the problem isn't teachers not caring enough. It's an education system designed to sort students rather than develop them. You can't teach your way out of a structure built on inequality.

The tech worker who got into the field to build tools that help people, now watching those tools extract data, manipulate behavior, and concentrate power. He's realized: the problem isn't individual engineers making unethical choices. It's a business model where surveillance and addiction are the product. You can't code your way out of a structure where user wellbeing and shareholder value are in direct conflict.

They're all hitting the same wall Ravi just hit: You can't solve systemic problems with individual solutions.

This is different from everything we've learned so far.

Matsya taught us discernment - to navigate the information flood. Essential. But what happens when the flood isn't natural but manufactured? When companies profit from confusion? When the business model requires keeping people disoriented?

Kurma taught us inner stability - to build foundation beneath chaos. Crucial. But what happens when the environment is deliberately designed to destabilize you? When apps are engineered to disrupt your attention? When the economy requires anxiety to function?

Varaha taught us to rescue what's buried - to reconnect with what sustains us. Necessary. But what happens when extraction is the economic engine? When protecting the environment conflicts with the fundamental logic of endless growth?

Narasimha taught us to resist tyranny - to confront abuse of power. Vital. But what happens when power isn't held by individual tyrants but embedded in systems? When algorithms oppress without anyone making a conscious choice to oppress?

Vamana taught us humility - to recognize our limits. Important. But what happens when those who control technology and wealth recognize no limits? When the system rewards ego and punishes humility?

Parashurama taught us to dismantle corruption - to tear down rot and rebuild. Essential. But what happens when corruption isn't in the system but is the system? When the "legitimate" functioning of institutions produces illegitimate outcomes?

Rama taught us integrity - to do what's right regardless of cost. Critical. But what happens when the system makes integrity nearly impossible? When doing right by your family means doing wrong by others, and the choices themselves are manufactured by structural inequality?

Krishna taught us to navigate impossible choices - to act with wisdom when there's no right answer. Profound. But what happens when impossible choices aren't rare dilemmas but daily realities? When the system creates them at industrial scale?

Buddha taught us to release craving - to find peace by letting go. Transformative. But what happens when the environment is engineered to manufacture craving? When the economy depends on dissatisfaction? When individual liberation has to fight against industrial-scale addiction engineering?

All of this wisdom is real. All of it matters. All of it is necessary.

But none of it is sufficient when the systems themselves are designed to create the very problems the wisdom addresses.

The Systems We've Built

Look at what we've actually constructed:

We've built an economic system that requires endless growth on a finite planet. That treats environmental destruction as "externalities" rather than costs. That measures success by GDP while the planet burns. We know this is insane. We have the technology and knowledge to build sustainable economies. But the system isn't designed for sustainability - it's designed for extraction and growth. You can't Varaha your way out of capitalism's fundamental logic.

We've built information systems that profit from confusion and manipulation. Platforms that make money by keeping you scrolling, by triggering outrage, by showing you content that confirms your biases and divides you from others. We know this is toxic. We could design systems that inform rather than manipulate. But the business model requires manipulation. You can't Matsya your way out of an advertising-based internet.

We've built healthcare systems that treat illness as a profit center rather than a problem to solve. That make money from keeping people dependent on medications rather than helping them get well. That price life-saving treatments based on what the market will bear rather than what it costs to produce. We know this is cruel. We could build systems that prioritize health. But the structure requires disease to be profitable. You can't Kurma your way out of healthcare capitalism.

We've built work systems that extract maximum productivity from people while providing minimum security. That treat workers as costs to minimize rather than humans to support. That automate jobs to increase shareholder value while leaving workers with no safety net. We know this is destructive. We could build economies that value human dignity. But the system is designed to maximize efficiency and profit, not wellbeing. You can't Vamana your way out of labor's devaluation.

We've built political systems where wealth translates directly into power. Where corporations write the laws that regulate them. Where the interests of capital override the needs of citizens. We know this is corrupt. We could build actual democracies. But the system concentrates power in the hands of those who benefit from concentration. You can't Parashurama or Narasimha your way out of plutocracy's gravity.

We've built technology systems that concentrate power in the hands of a few companies who control infrastructure, data, and algorithms that shape billions of lives. Where surveillance is the business model. Where AI development serves profit rather than human flourishing. We know this is dangerous. We could build technology for public good. But the system is designed to privatize gains and socialize harms. You can't regulate your way out when the regulators are captured by the regulated.

The pattern is clear: We've built systems optimized for extraction, concentration, and growth rather than for human and planetary flourishing.

And those systems create the crises we've been addressing. The misinformation isn't accidental - it's profitable. The mental health epidemic isn't random - it's generated by environments designed to be destabilizing. The environmental destruction isn't a mistake - it's the logical outcome of extractive economics. The inequality isn't unfortunate - it's how the system is designed to work.

Ravi sees this now. You can write perfect regulations for AI and they'll be circumvented, captured, or rendered obsolete because the system that creates and deploys AI is designed to maximize profit and power, not to serve human needs.

The climate scientist sees this. You can publish perfect research about renewable energy and it won't matter because the economic system runs on fossil fuels and changing that requires changing the economy itself, not just the energy source.

The healthcare worker sees this. You can provide perfect care and it won't change that the system makes money from sick people, not healthy ones.

The teacher sees this. You can be a perfect educator and it won't change that the system is designed to reproduce inequality, not eliminate it.

The Question We're Avoiding

Here's what makes this crisis different from all the others: It requires us to question the systems we've built and ask if they can be reformed or need to be replaced.

That's uncomfortable. Those systems provide our jobs, our security, our sense of how the world works. Questioning them feels radical, dangerous, impossible.

But what's the alternative? Keep using individual wisdom to navigate systems designed to make navigation nearly impossible? Keep practicing Rama's integrity in structures that punish integrity? Keep trying Buddha's peace in environments engineered to prevent peace?

At some point, compassion requires not just helping people swim against the current, but questioning why the current is so strong and whether it needs to flow in a different direction.

Ravi sits in that hearing room understanding: The question isn't how to make AI serve people within capitalism. The question is: What economic system would allow AI to actually serve people? What political system would make democratic governance of technology possible? What values need to change for technology to be designed for flourishing rather than extraction?

The climate scientist asks: What if we built an economy that treated planetary boundaries as real rather than as constraints to overcome? What would that actually look like?

The healthcare worker asks: What if we built a system that made money from health rather than from illness? How would that fundamentally change healthcare?

The teacher asks: What if we built an education system designed to develop every child's potential rather than to sort winners from losers? What would that require?

These aren't questions with easy answers. They're questions that require imagination, courage, and the willingness to build something fundamentally different from what we have.

This is what Kalki represents. Not another wisdom for navigating the world as it is, but the courage to transform the world into what it needs to become.

The ancient tradition understood this. Kalki isn't just another avatar teaching another truth. Kalki is the avatar of endings and beginnings. The one who comes when an age has run its course and needs to end for something new to begin.

We're living in that moment. The systems we've built have created abundance and innovation, yes. But they've also created the climate crisis, the inequality crisis, the mental health crisis, the meaning crisis, the democratic crisis. The age they represent is ending whether we're ready or not.

The question is: What do we build next?

The Avatar Who Hasn't Come Yet

Unlike the nine avatars before him, Kalki's story hasn't happened. It's prophecy, not history. Promise, not memory.

In the ancient texts, Kalki is described as the tenth and final avatar of Vishnu. He appears at the end of Kal Yug - the age of darkness, corruption, and decline. When *dharma* (righteousness, cosmic order, the way things should be) has degraded to its lowest point. When the systems meant to support human flourishing have become systems of exploitation and harm. When what was built to serve life has become what destroys it.

That's when Kalki comes.

Not to preserve the age, but to end it. Not to reform corruption, but to destroy it entirely. Not to help people navigate the broken world, but to break the broken world so something new can be built.

The image is stark: Kalki riding a white horse, wielding a blazing sword. Not the gentle teacher, the patient guide, the wise counselor. But the warrior who comes when teaching, guiding, and counseling are no longer enough. When the rot is so deep that cutting it out is the only path to healing.

This is uncomfortable. We want transformation to be gentle, gradual, consensual. We want change that doesn't disrupt, progress that doesn't destroy anything we value, evolution that keeps all the good parts of the old while adding new ones.

But sometimes transformation requires endings. Sometimes you can't build the new on top of the old. Sometimes the foundation itself is corrupt and needs to be demolished before anything sound can be constructed.

What the Prophecy Says

The texts describe Kal Yug - the age Kalki ends - in terms that sound eerily familiar:

Truth becomes rare. Lies proliferate to the point where no one can tell what's real. Does this sound like our information environment, where AI-generated deepfakes and algorithmic manipulation make truth nearly impossible to discern?

Wealth concentrates in the hands of a few while the many struggle. Power becomes hereditary. The gap between rich and poor becomes unbridgeable. Does this sound like our economy, where a handful of tech billionaires control more wealth than billions of people combined?

People become addicted to sense pleasures, unable to find satisfaction, constantly craving more. Does this sound like our culture of consumption and digital addiction, where we can't put down our phones even when our children need us?

Sacred institutions become corrupt, serving those in power rather than those they were meant to serve. Does this sound like our captured regulatory agencies, our pay-to-play politics, our healthcare systems that profit from illness?

The environment becomes polluted, resources are extracted without thought for tomorrow, and the very systems that sustain life are degraded. Does this sound like our climate crisis, our poisoned waters, our dying ecosystems?

In this age, according to the texts, even the wisest teachings become insufficient. People know what's right but lack the power to do it. The systems are too strong, the corruption too deep, the momentum too overwhelming.

That's when Kalki appears. Not with another teaching, not with more wisdom about how to be good within a bad system. But with the sword that cuts through the system itself.

The Courage to End

What makes Kalki's story so important - and so difficult - is what it says about endings.

We're taught to fix things, to reform them, to make them better. And that's right - most of the time. You don't burn down your house because one room needs renovation.

But what if the foundation is cracked? What if the structure itself is unsound? What if trying to fix it piece by piece just postpones the inevitable collapse and makes it more dangerous when it finally comes?

Kalki represents the wisdom to know when something can be reformed and when it needs to end. The courage to let go of what's familiar but broken, even when you don't know exactly what will replace it. The faith that transformation is possible even when it requires destruction of what is.

This isn't about violence or chaos. The sword Kalki wields isn't meant to harm people - it's meant to cut through systems that harm people. To end structures that have outlived their purpose. To clear space for something new to grow.

Think about it in nature. A forest fire seems destructive. It burns everything. But it's also how new growth begins. The old trees that blocked the light, that consumed all the nutrients, that prevented young trees from growing - they need to die for the forest to renew itself. The fire is terrifying. It's also necessary.

Kalki is the fire that clears the ground.

Why This Avatar Is Different

The first nine avatars worked within their ages. They preserved, protected, guided, fought, taught. They helped people navigate their worlds, even when those worlds were difficult.

Kalki is different. Kalki says: This world, this age, this way of organizing human life - it needs to end.

Not because people are bad. But because the systems have become so corrupt that trying to be good within them is like trying to swim upstream in a waterfall. You might make progress for a moment, but the current is overwhelming and you're fighting a battle you can't win.

Matsya helped you navigate the flood. Kalki asks: Why is there a flood? What if we need different systems for managing information, systems not designed to profit from confusion?

Kurma helped you build inner stability. Kalki asks: Why do you need heroic stability? What if we need environments designed for human wellbeing rather than designed to destabilize you for profit?

Varaha helped you rescue what's buried. Kalki asks: Why does it keep getting buried? What if we need economic systems that treat the environment as foundational rather than exploitable?

Narasimha helped you resist tyranny. Kalki asks: Why does tyranny keep emerging? What if we need political systems where power actually serves people rather than concentrating in the hands of a few?

And so on through all nine avatars. Each offers essential wisdom. Each is necessary. But all of them assume you're working within fundamentally sound systems that have been corrupted and can be restored.

Kalki asks: What if the systems themselves are the problem? What if they're working exactly as designed, and the design is what needs to change?

The Promise and the Challenge

Here's what makes Kalki both terrifying and hopeful:

Terrifying because endings are scary. Even when you know something is broken, letting it end feels like loss. The systems we have, however flawed, are familiar. We know how to navigate them. We've built our lives around them. Imagining their end means imagining uncertainty, disruption, the loss of what's known.

Hopeful because endings make beginnings possible. You can't build a just economy on top of an extractive one. You can't build democratic technology governance within plutocracy. You can't build sustainable systems within structures designed for endless growth. At some point, transformation requires the courage to end what is so something new can begin.

Kalki represents that courage.

The prophecy says Kalki hasn't come yet. The tenth avatar is still waiting. The age hasn't ended.

But here's the thing about prophecy - it's not prediction of what will happen. It's vision of what could happen. It's not fate, but possibility.

Kalki doesn't come from outside to save us. Kalki is what we become when we find the courage to transform the systems that need transformation. When we stop asking "how do I navigate this broken system" and start asking "how do we build a system that doesn't need to be broken?"

Every person who looks at AI and asks "what system would make this serve people rather than extract from them?" is channeling Kalki's energy.

Every climate activist who demands not just renewable energy but an economy that doesn't require endless growth is embodying Kalki's courage.

Every healthcare worker who fights not just for better insurance policies but for systems designed around health rather than profit is carrying Kalki's sword.

Every teacher who challenges not just this policy but the fundamental purpose of education in an unequal society is doing Kalki's work.

Every worker who organizes not just for better wages but for democratic ownership of the means of production is preparing Kalki's ground.

The Question Kalki Asks

Ravi sits in that hearing room realizing he's spent three years trying to make a fundamentally broken system slightly less broken. And Kalki's question echoes:

What if you stopped trying to fix it and started imagining what should replace it?

What if instead of asking "how do we regulate AI within capitalism" you asked "what economic system would make AI actually serve human flourishing?"

What if instead of accepting that systems create impossible choices, you asked "what systems would create possible choices?"

What if instead of teaching people to swim heroically against overwhelming currents, you asked "how do we change the course of the river?"

That's the courage Kalki represents. Not the courage to endure what's broken. The courage to end it and build something new.

The sword that cuts through what no longer serves life, so that life can flourish again.

When Endings Become Beginnings

Ravi closes his laptop and walks out of the hearing room. It's midnight now. The building is empty except for security.

He's done. Not with the work - but with this approach to it.

Three years he's been writing regulations, consulting with stakeholders, trying to make the system work. Three years of believing that if he could just get the framework right, if he could just balance all the interests correctly, if he could just think through all the edge cases - then AI could be governed responsibly within the existing system.

Tonight's testimony shattered that belief.

Not because anyone said anything shocking. But because everyone - the CEO, the researcher, the labor organizer, the civil rights advocate - all said the same thing in different ways: The system is working exactly as designed. The design is the problem.

The CEO follows every regulation while still deploying harmful AI. Because the regulations allow it. The regulations were written to allow it. The system isn't broken - it's functioning perfectly to prioritize profit over people.

The researcher watches AI advance faster than any regulatory process can keep up with. You're regulating last year's technology while this year's technology creates risks no one anticipated. You're playing catch-up with a player that's accelerating away from you.

The labor organizer sees workers treated as collateral damage. The system isn't failing to protect them - the system is designed to sacrifice them for efficiency.

The civil rights advocate points out that AI bias reflects societal bias. You can't fix biased AI without fixing the biased society that creates it.

Ravi has been trying to write better rules for a game that's rigged. And he just realized: you can't un-rig a rigged game by writing better rules. You need a different game.

The Realization

This is what Kalki's moment feels like. Not a dramatic revelation, but a quiet understanding that changes everything.

Ravi thinks about all the wisdom he's gathered through this work. He's learned Matsya's discernment - he can tell truth from spin, see through corporate PR, identify what actually matters in testimony. He's built Kurma's stability - he can stay grounded through contentious hearings, maintain perspective when things get chaotic. He's tried to protect what Varaha values - human dignity, democratic governance, public good.

He's resisted what Narasimha would resist - corporate capture, regulatory abuse, concentration of power. He's practiced Vamana's humility - acknowledged what he doesn't know, stayed open to learning. He's had Parashurama's persistence - worked year after year on incremental reforms. He's maintained Rama's integrity - refused to take industry money, called out corruption when he saw it.

He's navigated Krishna's impossible choices - balancing innovation and safety, progress and precaution, different stakeholders' competing needs. He's tried to practice Buddha's peace - released attachment to specific outcomes, found equanimity in uncertainty.

All of it necessary. All of it real. All of it insufficient.

Because he's been using all that wisdom to navigate a system designed to make navigation nearly impossible. He's been swimming against a current engineered to drown him. He's been trying to reform structures built to resist reform.

What Needs to Change

The question isn't "how do we regulate AI within capitalism?" The question is: "what economic system would allow AI to actually serve people?"

The question isn't "how do we balance innovation and safety?" The question is: "who gets to decide what innovation means and who it serves?"

The question isn't "how do we make this hearing more effective?" The question is: "what democratic processes would actually govern technology?"

These are different questions. They require different answers. They point toward transformation, not regulation.

Ravi walks to his car. Tomorrow morning there will be another hearing. More testimony. More proposed regulations that tinker at the edges while the core problems accelerate.

He could keep showing up to those hearings. Keep drafting those regulations. Keep trying to make the system work slightly better. It's legitimate work. Every harm prevented matters. Every protection that helps even one person matters.

But he knows now that it's not enough. That the gap between incremental reform and necessary transformation is too large to bridge. That his considerable expertise, his political relationships, his three years of learning - all of it could be redirected toward building what should exist rather than patching what can't work.

The Choice

This is Kalki's offer. Not to everyone at once, but to each person who sees clearly enough: the system is broken by design, and fixing it requires changing the design itself.

Not through violence. Not through chaos. But through the courage to say: this approach has run its course. This system cannot deliver what it promises. We need to build something different.

For Ravi, that might mean leaving government to work with movements building democratic governance of technology. Or staying in government but shifting his focus from regulation to democratization - public ownership of AI infrastructure, commons-based data systems, technology development accountable to communities rather than shareholders.

He doesn't know exactly what it looks like yet. But he knows what it isn't: more hearings about how to make extractive technology slightly less extractive. More regulations written within frameworks that assume corporate profit as the baseline. More years trying to patch a system designed to resist the very protections people need.

The age is ending whether we acknowledge it or not. The systems we've built have created abundance for some and crisis for many. The climate emergency accelerates. Inequality grows. Democratic institutions hollow out. Technology develops without democratic input or accountability.

Kalki doesn't promise that transformation will be easy or painless. Doesn't promise you'll know exactly what to build before you start building. Doesn't promise the new systems won't have their own problems.

But Kalki promises this: sometimes the most compassionate act isn't helping people swim better against overwhelming currents. It's changing the course of the river itself.

And that work begins with people like Ravi - people inside systems who understand them well enough to know they can't be fixed, who have skills and knowledge to redirect toward building alternatives, who find the courage to say: I'm done tinkering. I'm ready to transform.

The transformation is already beginning. Not in one place, but in thousands. Worker cooperatives building democratic ownership. Commons movements protecting shared resources. Communities creating participatory governance. Movements demanding not just better policies but different systems.

Ravi can join that work. Can bring his expertise to efforts already underway. Can help build what AI governance could look like if it served human flourishing rather than corporate profit.

Or he can keep doing what he's been doing - making marginal improvements to a fundamentally flawed system, hoping that somehow, eventually, incremental reform will be enough.

He gets in his car. Drives home. Tomorrow he'll decide what actually choosing transformation looks like for him.

But tonight, he knows: the work that brought him here taught him what doesn't work. The work ahead requires building what does.

That's Kalki's wisdom. Not destruction for its own sake. But the courage to end what cannot be saved so something better can begin.

What Kalki Would Do Today

Three weeks after that midnight realization, Ravi is sitting in a coffee shop with Angelina. She runs a nonprofit working on democratic governance of AI. He's been following her work for a year, impressed by how clearly she sees what he's only just understood: you can't regulate your way to accountability when the entire system is designed to evade accountability.

"I want to help," he tells her. "I don't know exactly how yet. But I'm done trying to reform what can't be reformed."

Angelina nods. She's heard this before - people hitting the wall, realizing that their expertise has been used to legitimize systems they meant to constrain. "What made you see it?"

"A hearing," Ravi says. "Everyone testified that the system is working exactly as designed. And I realized - I've been trying to redesign it from within, but I don't have the power to change the design. The people who do have that power benefit from the current design. So why would they let me change it?"

This is where transformation begins. Not with a grand plan, but with a clear-eyed recognition: **the system is the problem, and you can't fix it by working within its logic.**

Seeing What You're Actually Dealing With

For three years, Ravi called his work "AI governance." That framing made it sound neutral - just figuring out how to govern technology responsibly.

But that wasn't what he was doing. He was trying to make AI serve public good within capitalism - an economic system designed to maximize private profit. He was trying to create democratic oversight within plutocracy - a political system where wealth translates directly to power. He was trying to ensure fairness within structures built on inequality.

Once he names it clearly - "I'm trying to regulate AI within capitalism, and capitalism requires AI to maximize profit, not serve people" - the futility becomes obvious.

This is Kalki's first teaching: **name the system you're dealing with.** Not with vague language that makes you feel better, but with accuracy that lets you see clearly.

Not "the system has problems" but "capitalism's logic applied to AI means AI will be optimized for extraction, not flourishing."

Not "we need better oversight" but "regulatory capture means the industry controls its own oversight, so oversight serves the industry, not the public."

Not "AI has unintended consequences" but "AI is working exactly as intended - to maximize profit for shareholders - and the consequences are features, not bugs."

You can't transform what you can't see clearly. And you can't see clearly if you're using language designed to obscure.

Finding Your People

Angelina's organization has been working on AI governance alternatives for five years. Democratic ownership of AI infrastructure. Community control of algorithms that affect people's lives. Technology development accountable to those it impacts, not just those who profit from it.

They've built working models. Small scale, but functional. Proof that different approaches are possible.

"Why haven't I heard about this work?" Ravi asks.

"Because the people with platforms don't want you to know alternatives exist," Angelina says. "If you know cooperative ownership works, you start asking why we don't use it. If you know democratic governance of technology is possible, you start demanding it. The system survives by making alternatives invisible."

This is Kalki's second teaching: **you're not starting from scratch.** People have been building alternatives for decades, centuries. They've been doing the work while everyone else was trying to reform unreformable systems.

Your job isn't to invent transformation. It's to find the people already doing it and join them.

Ravi has expertise in policy, relationships with lawmakers, understanding of how government works. Angelina's organization needs exactly that. Not to write more regulations, but to help craft legislation for public ownership. Not to advise companies on compliance, but to help communities demand accountability.

He has leverage he didn't know he had. Not within the system he was trying to reform, but in movements trying to build alternatives to that system.

Building, Not Just Critiquing

Six months in, Ravi is helping draft a municipal bill for democratic governance of AI used in city services. It's small scale - just one city, just public sector AI. But it's real. If it passes, it'll be the first example of citizens having actual say in how algorithms that affect them are designed and deployed.

It's harder than writing regulations. Regulations work within existing power structures - you just have to convince people to accept constraints on their power (which they usually won't, but at least the path is clear). Building democratic structures means creating new power relationships from scratch.

But it's also more honest. He's not pretending that corporate-controlled AI can be made to serve public good through the right rules. He's helping build systems where public good is the actual goal, not a constraint on profit maximization.

This is Kalki's third teaching: **transformation requires creation, not just criticism.**

It's easy to say what's wrong. It's necessary to say what's wrong. But it's not sufficient.

You need to build what should exist. Even imperfectly. Even at small scale. Even knowing it might fail.

Because building proves that alternatives are possible. Every worker cooperative that succeeds shows that democratic ownership works. Every community land trust demonstrates that housing doesn't have to be wealth extraction. Every participatory budgeting process shows that real democracy is possible.

And because building gives people something to join. Critique without construction just makes people feel helpless. "The system is broken and we're trapped in it" leads to despair. "The system is broken and we're building alternatives" leads to action.

Accepting the Timeline

A year in, the municipal bill hasn't passed yet. It's stalled in committee. Corporate lobbyists are fighting it. The mayor is wavering under pressure.

Ravi is frustrated. He spent three years on regulatory work that accomplished little. Now he's spending his time on transformation work that's also slow.

"This is generational work," Angelina reminds him. "We're not going to replace capitalism with economic democracy in our lifetime. We're going to build examples, prove viability, create pressure, shift what's possible. Our grandchildren might live in the world we're working toward."

This is brutal honesty. But it's also liberating.

If Ravi expected transformation to be quick, he'd burn out when it's slow. If he accepts it's generational work, he can pace himself. Find joy in small victories. Celebrate a bill that advances out of committee even if it doesn't pass. Build relationships that will outlast any single campaign.

This is Kalki's fourth teaching: **transformation takes longer than you want it to.**

Not because people are slow or lazy. Because systems have momentum. Because power resists change. Because building new structures while old ones still dominate is hard.

You're planting trees whose shade you won't sit under. You're starting changes your children might complete. You're part of a movement that's longer than your lifetime.

That's not pessimism. It's reality. And accepting it makes the work sustainable.

Integrating All the Wisdom

The municipal bill creates impossible choices. If they include strong accountability mechanisms, corporate AI providers won't bid on city contracts. If they make it too easy for companies, they're not actually creating democratic governance.

Krishna's wisdom: navigate the complexity without demanding purity. Build what you can build, knowing it's imperfect.

The political fight means confronting power - tech companies threaten to pull out of the city if the bill passes. Narasimha's courage: resist the threats, call the bluff, don't let power veto accountability.

Ravi needs to maintain his integrity - not compromise core principles for political expediency. Rama's teaching: know your lines before you reach them.

He needs to stay grounded when the work is chaotic. Kurma's stability: build inner foundation that holds when external circumstances don't.

He needs to persist when progress is slow. Parashurama's commitment: keep showing up, year after year, even when you're not winning.

He needs humility about what he doesn't know. Vamana's teaching: this is new territory, stay open to learning, don't pretend certainty.

He needs to release attachment to specific outcomes. Buddha's peace: you can't control whether the bill passes, only whether you do the work with integrity.

He needs to discern what matters. Matsya's wisdom: which battles are worth fighting, which compromises are acceptable, what actually serves the goal.

He needs to protect what's worth protecting. Varaha's care: some parts of existing systems carry wisdom - preserve what should survive transformation.

All ten avatars. Not one at a time, but integrated. Each supporting the others. Each providing what the others can't.

Knowing the Limits

Two years in, the bill passes. Modified, not as strong as they hoped, but real. The city has democratic governance of AI in public services. Citizens have input. There's accountability.

It's a victory. A small one in a large system. One city, not the whole country. Public sector, not private. But real.

And Ravi knows: this doesn't solve the systemic problems. AI companies still extract wealth, concentrate power, operate without democratic input in private markets. The economic system still prioritizes profit over people.

Kalki's transformation helps build alternatives. But those alternatives exist within a larger system that actively works against them. The municipal bill is great - and it's also vulnerable to being undermined by state legislation, corporate pressure, future administrations.

This is why transformation is ongoing work. Why you don't build one alternative and declare victory. Why the work Ravi is doing now is part of a much longer struggle.

He needs continued resistance (Narasimha) to protect what's been built. Continued persistence (Parashurama) to keep building when progress is slow. Continued wisdom (Krishna) to navigate setbacks. Continued peace (Buddha) to sustain himself for long work.

And he needs to remember: he's part of a movement. Not the movement. One person doing one piece of work that connects to thousands of people doing thousands of pieces. Together, they're building the world that should exist.

The Work Continues

Ravi still goes to hearings sometimes. But his role has changed. He's not there to write regulations anymore. He's there to testify about alternatives. To make visible what the system tries to keep invisible. To say clearly: regulation within this system isn't enough, we need different systems.

He's found his people. He's doing the work. He's accepted the timeline. He's integrated the wisdom.

This is what Kalki offers: not a blueprint for transformation, but the courage to begin it. Not certainty about what comes next, but clarity about what can't continue. Not the promise of quick victory, but the strength for long struggle.

The transformation is already happening. The question is whether you're part of it.

For Ravi, the answer is yes. And that makes all the difference.

What Kalki Cannot Do Alone

Kalki gives us something essential: the courage to end what's broken and build something new. The vision to see that some problems aren't solved by navigating systems but by transforming them. The willingness to accept endings as necessary for beginnings.

But sit with transformation for a moment, and you see why Kalki alone would be dangerous.

A sword that cuts through systems without Matsya's discernment could destroy what should be preserved. How do you know which parts of the old system carry wisdom worth keeping and which parts are truly corrupt? Without discernment, transformation becomes destruction without purpose.

Transformation without Kurma's stability creates chaos that people can't sustain. If you tear down structures without helping people build inner foundation first, you leave them adrift. The instability can be worse than the broken system it replaced.

Transformation without Varaha's care for what sustains life risks destroying the very things we need to survive. Not everything old is corrupt. Some ancient wisdom, some traditional practices, some natural systems - they need protection even during radical change.

Transformation without Narasimha's fierce resistance to power means those who benefit from the old system will simply capture the new one. You can build beautiful alternatives, and if you don't confront existing power, they'll be co-opted or crushed.

Transformation without Vamana's humility becomes arrogant certainty that you know exactly what should replace what was. But you don't. No one does. Humility about your limits is essential when building something new.

Transformation without Parashurama's sustained commitment fades when the initial energy wanes. Tearing down is often easier than building up. Without persistence, you get destruction without reconstruction.

Transformation without Rama's integrity becomes "the ends justify the means." If you abandon principles while pursuing transformation, you risk creating systems as corrupt as the ones you're replacing, just with different beneficiaries.

Transformation without Krishna's wisdom creates more impossible choices than it solves. Change is complex. There are no perfect options. Without the ability to navigate ambiguity, transformation movements split into factions demanding purity that can't exist.

Transformation without Buddha's peace burns people out. If you can't find equanimity in uncertainty, can't release attachment to specific outcomes, can't sustain yourself for long work - you'll exhaust yourself and everyone around you.

This is why the tenth avatar doesn't replace the first nine. This is why Kalki is the completion, not the culmination.

You need all ten. Together. At once. Each providing what the others cannot.

Ravi's courage to transform AI governance systems means nothing if he doesn't:

- Discern truth from manipulation in a world of AI-generated content (Matsya)
- Maintain inner stability while doing uncertain, difficult work (Kurma)
- Protect human dignity and planetary boundaries during technological change (Varaha)
- Resist corporate capture of whatever new systems he helps build (Narasimha)
- Stay humble about not having all answers (Vamana)
- Persist year after year when progress is slow (Parashurama)
- Maintain integrity when pressured to compromise (Rama)
- Navigate the complex trade-offs transformation creates (Krishna)
- Find peace with imperfect progress (Buddha)

Remove any one of these, and transformation either fails or becomes destructive.

This is the insight we've been building toward through every chapter, every limitation, every recognition that one avatar's wisdom isn't enough:

The avatars need each other. Not sequentially, but simultaneously. Not as alternatives, but as complements. Not competing approaches, but integrated wisdom.

You can't pick and choose. You can't say "I'll take Kalki's transformation and Krishna's wisdom but skip Vamana's humility." The wisdom is a whole. Each piece essential. Each supporting the others.

Matsya without Kalki means navigating forever without addressing why the flood exists. Kalki without Matsya means transformation without knowing what's worth preserving.

Kurma without Kalki means building stability within broken systems. Kalki without Kurma means change that people can't sustain.

The same is true for every pairing. Each avatar addresses something the others don't. Each provides wisdom essential for the others to work.

This is what the ancient tradition understood when it taught about ten avatars, not one. Not because Vishnu couldn't get it right the first time, but because reality requires ten kinds of wisdom, each essential, each incomplete without the others.

Ravi needs all ten. So does the climate scientist, the healthcare worker, the teacher, every person trying to both navigate and transform the world.

The question isn't which avatar you need. It's how you integrate all ten - how you hold discernment and transformation, stability and change, protection and courage, resistance and humility, persistence and wisdom, integrity and complexity, peace and action - all at once, each informing the others.

That's the synthesis we need. That's the wisdom for our age.

Not one avatar. All ten. Together.

* * *

<h1 style="text-align:center">11</h1>

All Ten Together

The call comes at 4:47am.

Satya fumbles for his phone in the dark, already knowing it's bad. Good news doesn't call before dawn.

"Mayor." It's Linda from the fire service. Her voice is tight. "The wind shifted. The Coldwater Fire jumped the containment line. It's moving toward town faster than the models predicted. We're looking at 18-24 hours, maybe less."

Satya sits up. His wife Priya is already awake beside him, reading his face.

"How fast?"

"If the wind holds, it'll reach the eastern ridge by tomorrow afternoon. From there to the town center - maybe six hours. We need to start evacuation now."

Eighteen hours. Maybe less. To evacuate 14,000 people from a mountain town with two roads out, during peak summer tourist season when the population is closer to 20,000.

He's been mayor of Cedar Falls for two years. Before that, he taught high school history for fifteen years. He ran for mayor because the previous administration had let the town council become a rubber stamp for development interests, and someone needed to care about the actual community.

He never imagined this.

"I'm on my way," he says.

Hour 1: When Information Is Chaos

By 6am, Satya is in the emergency operations center - a conference room in the town hall that's been converted into crisis headquarters. Maps cover the walls. Screens show satellite imagery of the fire. The room fills quickly: fire chief, police chief, public works director, emergency services coordinator, county officials joining by video.

And immediately, Satya is drowning in conflicting information.

The fire service says evacuate everyone now. The county says staged evacuation - elderly and vulnerable first, then expanding zones. The state fire coordinator on the video call says the wind models might change, the fire might slow, don't create unnecessary panic.

The local news is broadcasting footage from the eastern ridge - flames visible on the horizon. Social media is exploding with rumors: the fire is already at the ridge, the roads are blocked, the bridges are going to be destroyed, the town is doomed.

His phone buzzes constantly. Town council members. Business owners. The regional tourism board saying evacuation will devastate the summer economy. A state representative saying don't overreact, remember what happened to Redwood when they evacuated unnecessarily and it cost millions.

Satya feels Matsya's challenge viscerally. The flood of information. Truth mixed with lies mixed with outdated data mixed with speculation mixed with agenda. He needs to see clearly - what's signal, what's noise, what's actual threat versus what's fear versus what's manipulation.

Linda lays out the facts as she knows them: Fire is 12 miles out, moving at approximately half a mile per hour with current winds. Wind forecast is uncertain - might increase, might decrease. If it increases, they have less time. If it decreases, they have more. The containment line failed because it was based on old forest density maps that didn't account for drought conditions.

Satya asks the question that matters: "What's your professional assessment? Not the models, not the maybe. What do you think?"

Linda meets his eyes. "I think we evacuate. Now. I think if we wait and I'm right, people die. If we evacuate and I'm wrong, we've inconvenienced people and spent money. I'd rather be wrong and everyone's alive."

Matsya's discernment: Cut through the noise. Preserve what actually matters. Trust the people who know, not the people who speculate.

"We evacuate," Satya says. "Full town, starting now."

Hour 3: When Everything Destabilizes

By 8am, the evacuation order is public and everything is chaos.

The police chief reports gridlock on both highways out of town. People are panicking. Two accidents already. One family's car broke down and they're blocking a lane. The gas stations are mobbed - lines stretching blocks. The grocery stores are being stripped. Someone pulled a gun on someone else who tried to cut in line.

Satya's phone is ringing nonstop. Angry calls. Scared calls. The hospital administrator saying they can't evacuate all the patients in time. The nursing home director saying the same. The owner of the Cedar Falls Inn saying he has 200 guests who are demanding refunds. A town council member saying this is political suicide, he'll be blamed if the fire doesn't actually hit.

Priya texts: *The kids' school is in chaos. Teachers don't know if they should evacuate or shelter. Parents are pulling kids out mid-class. Do I bring them home or leave them there?*

Satya feels like the ground beneath him is cracking. This is Kurma's crisis - everything external is falling apart. The stability he thought existed (orderly evacuation, people following instructions, systems working) is revealed as illusion.

He needs foundation beneath the chaos. Internal stability when external circumstances are collapsing.

He closes his eyes for ten seconds. Breathes. Remembers why he's here. Not to be popular. Not to avoid blame. To keep people alive.

He opens his eyes. Starts making calls.

To the hospital: Yes, evacuate critical patients now, we'll coordinate ambulances. Stable patients shelter in place for now, we'll revisit in two hours.

To the nursing home: Same. Critical residents go now. Others prepare but stay for now unless fire speed changes.

To the police: Set up traffic control at all major intersections. One officer per gas station to prevent violence. No cutting in lines. Anyone who threatens others gets arrested on the spot.

To Priya: *Bring the kids home. We stay together.*

To his assistant: Schedule a public address in one hour. Livestream it. He needs to speak directly to people.

Kurma's teaching: You can't control the chaos. You can find ground within yourself that holds when nothing else does.

Hour 6: When You Must Protect What Matters

By 11am, Satya is facing a choice he never wanted to make.

The eastern neighborhoods - the ones closest to the fire - are evacuating too slowly. People are trying to pack entire houses. Loading furniture, photos, valuables. The roads out are clogged with moving trucks.

His public works director reports: "If everyone keeps evacuating like this, we'll have gridlock by mid-afternoon. The western neighborhoods won't be able to get out. And if the fire moves faster than we think..."

"What do you need me to do?"

"Tell people to leave now. Just get in their cars and go. Leave every-thing."

Satya knows what this means. He's asking people to abandon their homes, their possessions, their memories. Everything they've built. He's asking them to save their lives and lose everything else.

This is Varaha's demand: Rescue what actually sustains life. And recognize that things - however precious - aren't life.

He goes live on the town's emergency broadcast. His face on every screen, every phone, every computer.

"This is Mayor Satya. I need you to listen carefully. The fire is moving faster than we hoped. If you're in the eastern evacuation zone and you're still packing, stop. Get in your car right now. Take your family, your pets, whatever you can grab in five minutes. Leave everything else. Your life is worth more than your things."

He sees himself on the screen. He looks exhausted, scared, serious. Good. People need to see this is real.

"I know what I'm asking. I know you're losing things that matter. But here's the truth: If you don't leave now, you might not leave at all. And I care more about seeing you alive next week than I care about whether you saved your furniture."

Varaha's wisdom: Protect what's sacred. And be fierce about distinguishing what's sacred (life, people, dignity) from what's not (things, possessions, comfort).

Hour 9: When Power Tries to Override Safety

By 2pm, Satya is in a screaming match with someone who should be helping.

Councilman Morrison is on the phone, and he's furious. "You've shut down the entire town! Do you know what this costs? The summer revenue alone—"

"There's a fire—"

"—which might not even reach us! The state coordinator said the models are uncertain. You're destroying local business based on maybe. The lawsuit exposure alone—"

"People's lives—"

"—are not more important than their livelihoods!" Morrison is yelling now. "You think you're some kind of hero, but you're going to bankrupt this town. I'm calling an emergency council meeting to revoke the evacuation order."

Satya feels rage rising. This is Narasimha's moment - when power serves itself rather than people, when authority needs to be confronted, when abuse masquerades as practicality.

"You try that," Satya says quietly, "and I'll hold a press conference explaining that while people were evacuating, you were worried about tourism revenue. Let's see how that plays for your reelection."

"You're threatening me?"

"I'm telling you that I'm the mayor, I've declared an emergency, and the evacuation stands. You can challenge it after everyone's safe. Right now, you can help or get out of the way."

He hangs up.

His hands are shaking. He's never talked to Morrison like that. Never threatened anyone. But Morrison was trying to override safety for money, and Satya can't allow it.

Narasimha's teaching: Sometimes compassion requires fierce resistance. Sometimes protecting people means confronting power. Sometimes you have to bare your teeth.

Hour 10: When Integrity Has a Price

By 3pm, Satya faces a moment where telling the truth will cost him everything.

A reporter from the regional news calls. She's heard rumors that the town's emergency supplies are inadequate. That the warehouse was supposed to be full but isn't. That there might be corruption involved.

"Is it true, Mr. Mayor? Did someone steal disaster funds?"

Satya knows what happens if he tells the truth right now, in the middle of the crisis, on camera.

The town will look incompetent. His administration will be blamed - even though this happened before he took office. Morrison and others will use it to undermine him, to say he can't manage a crisis, to call for his resignation. The investigation he's planning will become a political weapon against him. His ability to lead through the rest of this emergency will be compromised.

The smart political move is to deflect. Say "we're focused on the immediate crisis, we'll address questions about preparedness after everyone's safe." Not a lie, just evasion. Protect his position, investigate quietly later, maintain authority to lead.

But the reporter is asking directly. And people deserve to know why the supplies they paid for aren't there. And Satya became mayor because he cared about truth, not because he wanted to be a politician who evaded it.

"Yes," he says. "The emergency warehouse was supposed to be stocked with $200,000 worth of supplies. Most of them aren't there. It appears the contractor billed us but didn't deliver. We're working with what we have, getting additional supplies from the county and Red Cross. And after this crisis is over, we'll investigate fully and hold people accountable."

"Whose responsibility—"

"Right now, my responsibility is keeping people alive. The accountability part comes after. But yes, the supplies should have been there, and they're not, and that's a failure I'm dealing with."

He hangs up knowing he just handed Morrison ammunition. Knowing the headlines will be brutal. Knowing his political future just got much harder.

But he looked at that question and knew: if he became the mayor who evaded truth to protect himself, he'd become exactly what he ran against. The cost of maintaining integrity is sometimes everything. You pay it anyway.

Rama's teaching: Integrity is what you do when doing right costs you everything you have. You don't evade the truth to protect your position. You tell the truth and accept the consequences.

Hour 12: When You Must Accept Limits

By 5pm, Satya is facing his own breaking point.

He's been awake for 13 hours. Making decisions constantly. Coordinating evacuations, managing resources, handling crises. He hasn't eaten. Hasn't sat down except in the car driving between locations. His assistant keeps handing him coffee.

And it's not enough. He can't be everywhere. Can't solve everything. Can't save everyone personally.

The nursing home director calls: "We need more ambulances. We have 15 residents who can't evacuate safely without medical transport, and you said we'd have ambulances, and we only have five."

Satya checks. The ambulances are all deployed. Some evacuating the hospital. Some responding to medical emergencies - heart attacks from stress, a car accident, someone fell while packing and broke their hip.

"I don't have more ambulances," he says. "I'm sorry. I thought we would, but we don't."

"So what do we do?"

"Can any of them travel by car if we send volunteers with medical training?"

"Some. Not all."

"Then we move who we can move, and we shelter the rest in place with staff. I'll see if the county can send more ambulances, but I can't promise anything."

He hangs up feeling like he's failing. He's the mayor. He's supposed to have answers, resources, solutions. He doesn't.

This is Vamana's teaching, bitter and necessary: You have limits. Real ones. You can't save everyone yourself. You can't be everywhere. You can't solve every problem. Pretending otherwise doesn't help anyone.

He tells his assistant: "I need you to coordinate the nursing home situation. I trust you. I can't micromanage this and handle everything else."

Delegation isn't failure. Accepting limits isn't giving up. It's recognizing what's yours to do and what requires others.

Vamana's humility: Know your appropriate size. You're not the hero who saves everyone. You're one person doing your part in a larger effort.

Hour 16: When Past Corruption Creates Present Crisis

By 9pm, Satya is looking at maps with his fire chief, and he's learning how the current crisis was built by decisions made years ago.

Linda points to the eastern neighborhoods - the ones most at risk, the ones they evacuated first. "These subdivisions shouldn't exist," she says. "Five years ago, when the developers proposed them, fire services said no. Too close to the forest, too few access roads, high fire risk. We recommended denial."

"But they were built anyway."

"Town council overrode our recommendation. The development would bring property tax revenue, construction jobs, growth. The mayor at the time said we were being overly cautious, that modern building codes would handle fire risk. Council voted 4-1 to approve."

Satya feels sick. "How many homes?"

"Three hundred and forty-two. All in the highest risk zone. And because they were approved, other developers followed. The whole eastern corridor - it's all development that fire services said shouldn't be there."

"Who voted for it?"

Linda pulls up the old council minutes. Four names. One of them is Morrison - the councilman who tried to stop the evacuation today for economic reasons.

This is Parashurama's territory: Institutional corruption that looks legitimate on paper. A town council that put tax revenue over safety. Developers who knew the risk but built anyway because profit mattered more than people. A system that allowed it because growth was treated as inherently good.

And now, years later, it's not the councilmembers facing consequences. It's the 342 families who bought homes in what should never have been a neighborhood. It's the firefighters who have to risk their lives protecting structures that never should have existed.

"Can we do anything about this now?" Satya asks.

"No. The homes exist. People live there. We evacuate them and hope the fire doesn't reach them. But after this is over..." Linda looks at him directly. "The same developers are proposing three new subdivisions on the western ridge. Same problems, different location. Council meeting is scheduled for next month."

Satya nods slowly. "After this is over, we revisit the town's development policies. All of them. And we make sure fire safety isn't optional anymore."

Parashurama's wisdom: Sometimes you can't fix past corruption in the moment - you can only work around it and commit to dismantling it properly later. But that commitment matters. The work of accountability is ongoing, not one-time. You note it, you survive it, and then you systematically tear down the rot so it can't create the next crisis.

Hour 20: When Every Choice Violates Something Sacred

By 1am, Satya faces the decision he's been dreading.

The fire speed increased. Wind picked up. They have maybe six hours until it reaches the eastern ridge, six more until it reaches town. Twelve hours total if they're lucky.

They've evacuated 18,000 people. But about 2,000 are still in town. Some refused to leave (elderly residents who won't abandon homes, libertarians who don't trust government, people too poor to have cars or gas money). Some couldn't leave (the hospital patients and nursing home residents too critical to move, some people with disabilities, some people the system just missed).

And the roads out are at capacity. If they try to evacuate the remaining 2,000 now, they'll create gridlock that traps everyone - including the emergency responders, the police, the firefighters who need to stay until the last minute.

Fire chief: "We need to send the emergency personnel out soon. If they wait too long, they won't make it either."

Police chief: "We can't abandon 2,000 people."

County coordinator: "Maybe the fire will slow. Maybe the wind will shift. You don't know for certain—"

"Stop." Satya's voice cuts through. "I need everyone to be quiet for one minute."

The room goes silent.

He's facing Krishna's dilemma. Every option violates something sacred.

If he orders emergency personnel to evacuate now, they save themselves but abandon 2,000 people who will have no help, no protection, no rescue if things go wrong. Some of those people will die.

If he orders them to stay, they might all get trapped. The emergency responders, the police, the firefighters - they have families too. They deserve to live too. And if they die trying to save people who could have evacuated earlier but chose not to, who's responsible?

There is no right answer. There is no choice that honors all duties. His duty to protect everyone. His duty to not sacrifice the protectors for the protected. His duty to stay hopeful versus his duty to be realistic.

Krishna's teaching: When dharma conflicts with dharma, you act according to your best judgment of duty, knowing you'll cause harm either way, and release your attachment to knowing whether you chose correctly.

"Here's what we do," Satya says. "Emergency personnel who want to evacuate now can go. No judgment, no consequences. You have families, you have every right to survive. Those who choose to stay, we make one more sweep of the town, we help anyone who wants last-minute evacuation, and we prep shelter locations for anyone who's staying. At dawn, no matter what, remaining emergency personnel leave. And we hope the fire slows, and we hope the shelters hold, and we hope we've done enough."

Some personnel leave. Some stay. Satya doesn't judge either choice. Krishna taught Arjuna that both paths violated sacred obligations. Satya is learning the same lesson.

Hour 24: When You Can't Let Go

By 5am, Satya should leave.

The fire is six miles out. Moving slower than feared, but still moving. Dawn is coming. Most remaining emergency personnel are evacuating.

His assistant says, "Mayor, we need to go. You've done everything you can."

But Satya is standing in the town square, watching the sunrise paint the sky orange - or maybe that's smoke. He can't tell anymore.

He's texted Priya every hour. She's safe with the kids at her sister's place, three towns over. They're okay. He should go be with them.

But he keeps thinking: Did I miss someone? Is there a house I didn't check? A person who needed help? A decision I got wrong?

He's been running on adrenaline and coffee for 24 hours. Making life-and-death choices constantly. He can't stop. Can't rest. Can't accept that he's done all he can do.

This is Buddha's territory: The craving to control outcomes. The attachment to having saved everyone perfectly. The inability to release what you cannot control.

His assistant, Sarah, touches his shoulder. "Satya. You did everything humanly possible. Some things are beyond your control. The fire will do what the fire does. The people who stayed made their choices. You can't save everyone. And staying here won't change what happens."

"What if I missed someone?"

"Then you missed someone. And that's terrible. But you also saved 18,000 people who might have died if you hadn't acted fast, hadn't made hard calls, hadn't kept going when you were exhausted. You can't control the outcome. You can only control that you did your best."

Buddha's wisdom: Release attachment to outcomes you cannot control. Find peace not in having prevented all suffering, but in having acted according to your dharma with full awareness.

Satya gets in the car. Sarah drives. He watches the town disappear behind them in the rearview mirror.

He did his best. It might not be enough. He has to live with that.

Hour 36: When You See the System Itself Must Change

Twelve hours later, Satya is at the county evacuation center, watching the news.

The fire reached the eastern ridge. It's burning through the forest. But it slowed. The wind shifted. It's still a threat, but it's not the catastrophic worst-case scenario.

The town might survive. Most of it, anyway.

And Satya is looking at his phone, reading messages that make him want to scream.

The governor's office issued a statement: "We're grateful the fire was contained before reaching Cedar Falls. This demonstrates the effectiveness of our forest management policies."

The state fire coordinator is being interviewed: "Our models predicted the fire would slow, and they were correct. Evacuations should be based on data, not panic."

Councilman Morrison sent an email to local press: "While I appreciate Mayor Chen's caution, the economic cost of this evacuation was unnecessary. We need leadership that balances safety with practical concerns."

Satya reads these and realizes: They learned nothing.

The governor won't fund better forest management. The state coordinator won't improve their models (which were wrong). Morrison won't stop prioritizing money over lives. The contractor who stole disaster supplies won't face consequences unless Satya pushes it.

The system that created this crisis - the one that underfunded fire prevention, that allowed corrupt contractors, that prioritized development over safety, that treated disasters as PR opportunities - that system is still there. Still functioning exactly as designed.

Satya can be the best mayor possible. Can have perfect integrity, perfect judgment, perfect courage. Can make all the right calls. And still, the next mayor will face the same crisis because the system itself creates these crises.

This is Kalki's realization: Sometimes individual excellence isn't enough. Sometimes the system itself is broken and needs transformation, not just better people working within it.

Satya doesn't know yet what that transformation looks like. But he knows he can't go back to just trying to be a good mayor within a bad system. Something fundamental has to change.

Hour 48: All Ten Together

Two days later, the fire is contained. The town is still standing. People are starting to come home.

Satya is back in his office. Exhausted. Shaken. Changed.

Priya comes in with coffee. Sits across from him. "How are you?"

"I don't know," he says honestly. "I think I did okay. I think I made mostly right calls. But I also made calls that cost people. And I don't know if I could have done it differently."

"You used everything you knew," Priya says. "I was watching. You did."

And he realizes she's right. He did use everything.

Matsya's discernment when he was drowning in information and had to find truth.

Kurma's stability when everything was chaos and he needed ground beneath him.

Varaha's fierce protection when he had to tell people to choose life over possessions.

Narasimha's resistance when Morrison tried to override safety for money.

Vamana's humility when he had to accept his limits and delegate.

Parashurama's commitment to addressing corruption even while working around it.

Rama's integrity when every choice had a cost but he chose according to principle anyway.

Krishna's wisdom when he faced impossible choices between competing duties.

Buddha's peace when he had to release attachment to controlling outcomes.

Kalki's recognition that the system itself needs transformation.

He didn't use them one at a time. He used them all, constantly, flowing together. Each supporting the others. Each providing what the others couldn't.

And even with all ten, it was barely enough. If he'd been missing even one - if he'd lacked discernment or stability or courage or humility or persistence or integrity or wisdom or peace or transformative vision - something critical would have failed.

This is what the synthesis means. Not understanding the avatars intellectually. But living them. Integrating them. Needing all of them simultaneously because reality requires nothing less.

What All Ten Together Makes Possible

A week later, Satya calls a town meeting.

Cedar Falls lost some homes on the eastern edge. But the town stands. Most people are home. No one died.

And Satya has a proposal.

"We survived this fire," he says. "Barely. Because of luck, because of people's courage, because we made some decent calls. But we shouldn't need luck next time. We shouldn't need heroic efforts to avoid catastrophe. We should build systems that make safety normal, not emergency."

He lays out a plan: Real fire prevention. Funded disaster supplies with actual oversight. Community evacuation plans practiced before crisis hits. Emergency services that aren't chronically understaffed. And investigation of the contractor who stole from disaster funds.

Some of it he can do as mayor. Some requires county support. Some requires state policy change. Some requires years of work.

But it's possible. Because transformation isn't one dramatic moment. It's sustained effort, year after year, building what should exist.

And he's going to need all ten forms of wisdom to do it.

Discernment to see what's real. Stability to sustain himself through long work. Protection of what matters. Resistance to those who benefit from dysfunction. Humility about what he doesn't know. Persistence through setbacks. Integrity when pressured to compromise. Wisdom to navigate complexity. Peace with imperfect progress. And vision to transform rather than just manage.

All ten. Together. Not as separate teachings, but as integrated capacity for being fully human in a world that requires everything you have.

The Promise

This is what the avatars offer.

Not easy answers. Not guarantee of success. Not protection from hardship.

But complete wisdom for navigating and transforming a complex, broken, beautiful world.

Satya needed all ten avatars to lead his town through crisis. You will need all ten for whatever you're facing. Not might need. Will need.

Because your life isn't just one crisis. It's all of them, in different forms, at different times. You'll need to navigate information floods and maintain inner stability and protect what's sacred and resist tyranny and practice humility and persist through difficulty and maintain integrity and navigate impossible choices and find peace and work for transformation.

Not one at a time. All at once. Constantly. For the rest of your life.

The wisdom is ancient. The need is urgent. The integration is everything.

The gods haven't abandoned you. They're waiting to return - through you. Through the capacities you develop. Through the wisdom you integrate. Through the person you become when you stop choosing between them and start embodying all ten.

Matsya's discernment. Kurma's stability. Varaha's protection. Narasimha's courage. Vamana's humility. Parashurama's persistence. Rama's integrity. Krishna's wisdom. Buddha's peace. Kalki's transformation.

All ten. Together. Now.

That's what makes impossible things possible. What makes broken things healable. What makes you capable of facing whatever comes.

The question isn't whether you need all ten avatars.

The question is: Are you ready to begin developing them?

The work starts now.

* * *

About the Author

Darwin was born and raised in Agra, India, in a household steeped in Hindu tradition. His parents introduced him to the sacred texts, stories, and values of their faith from an early age — planting seeds that would quietly grow for decades. An Electronics Engineer by education, he has spent two decades in IT, and serves as a Senior Director at one of the leading life sciences consulting firms in the industry. Married with two sons, Darwin found that the ancient world never really left him. Over the years, he noticed a recurring pattern: the struggles he witnessed in modern life — whether in himself or in the world around him — seemed to echo the very crises that Lord Vishnu's avatars had once appeared to resolve. That persistent inner voice became this book.